The Triple Helix

A Triple Helix of university–industry–government interactions is the key to innovation in increasingly knowledge-based societies. As the creation, dissemination, and utilization of knowledge moves from the periphery to the center of industrial production and governance, the concept of innovation, in product and process, is itself being transformed. In its place is a new sense of "innovation in innovation"—the restructuring and enhancement of the organizational arrangements and incentives that foster innovation.

This Triple Helix intersection of relatively independent institutional spheres generates hybrid organizations such as technology transfer offices in universities, firms, and government research labs and business and financial support institutions such as angel networks and venture capital for new technology-based firms that are increasingly developing around the world.

The Triple Helix describes this new innovation model and assists students, researchers, and policy-makers in addressing such questions as: How do we enhance the role of universities in regional economic and social development? How can governments, at all levels, encourage citizens to take an active role in promoting innovation in innovation and, conversely, how can citizens so encourage their governments? How can firms collaborate with each other and with universities and government to become more innovative? What are the key elements and challenges to reaching these goals?

Henry Etzkowitz, PhD, holds the Chair in Management of Innovation, Creativity, and Enterprise and is Director of the Triple Helix Research Group, Newcastle University Business School, UK. He is also Visiting Research Professor, Department of Technology and Society, School of Engineering and Applied Sciences, Stony Brook University, USA.

The Triple Helix

University–Industry–Government
Innovation in Action

Henry Etzkowitz

Routledge
Taylor & Francis Group

NEW YORK AND LONDON

First published 2008
by Routledge
270 Madison Ave, New York, NY 10016

Simultaneously published in the UK
by Routledge
2 Park Square, Milton Park, Abingdon, Oxon OX14 4RN

*Routledge is an imprint of the Taylor & Francis Group, an
informa business*

© 2008 Henry Etzkowitz

Typeset in Sabon by
The Running Head Limited, www.therunninghead.com
Printed and bound in the United States of America on acid-free
paper by Sheridan Books, Inc.

Library of Congress Cataloging in Publication Data
Etzkowitz, Henry, 1940–
The triple helix: university-industry-government innovation / by Henry Etzkowitz.
    p. cm.
    Includes index.
1. Academic-industrial collaboration. 2. Public-private sector cooperation.
3. Research and development partnership. 4. Technological innovations.
5. Technology transfer. I. Title.
LC1085.E89 2008
338'.064—dc22

                                                    2007040853

ISBN10: 0–415–96450–4 (hbk)
ISBN 10: 0–415–96451–2 (pbk)
ISBN10: 0–203–92960–8 (ebk)

ISBN13: 978–0–415–96450–0 (hbk)
ISBN 13: 978–0–415–96451–7 (pbk)
ISBN13: 978–0–203–92960–5 (ebk)

For Alex

Contents

List of figures		ix
Acknowledgments		xi
	Introduction	1
1	Pathways to the triple helix	7
2	The entrepreneurial university	27
3	The evolution of the firm	43
4	The optimum role of government	59
5	Regional innovation	75
6	Triple helix technopolis	90
7	The incubation of innovation	105
8	Reinventing venture capital	122
9	The endless transition	137
	Notes	149
	Index	157

Figures

1.1   The statist model.   12
1.2   The laissez-faire model.   13
1.3   The social structure of the triple helix.   16
1.4   Triple helix field interaction model.   19
1.5   Synthetic interaction of triple helix.   20
1.6   Circulation of individuals in the triple helix.   21
1.7   Non-linear and netlike pentagonal model of technological
      innovation.   24
2.1   The evolution of university technology transfer capabilities.   36

Acknowledgments

My deepest appreciation to Dr Goran Arvidsson, of the Center for Business and Policy Studies (SNS), Stockholm, and Per Eriksson, Director of VINNOVA, Sweden's Innovation Systems Agency, who commissioned the original Swedish edition of *The Triple Helix*, and to Professor Chunyan Zhou of Shenyang University, who organized the Chinese edition.

My special thanks to cofounder of the Triple Helix international conference series Loet Leydesdorff and to Convenors José Carvello Mello, Merle Jacob, Mats Benner, Riccardo Viale, and Poh Kam Wong (Amsterdam, 1996; Purchase, New York, 1998; Rio de Janeiro, 2000; Copenhagen/Lund, 2002; Turin/Milan, 2005; and Singapore, 2007), and to the organizers of the predecessor series of university–industry meetings: Peter Healey, Andrew Webster, and Elsa Blum (Maratea, Italy, 1991; Purchase, New York, 1992; and Mexico City, 1993).

I wish to thank Tommy Berquist, SMI Consulting; Magnus Klofsten, Linköping University; and Devrim Goktepe, Lund University, for comments. Warm regards to colleagues in the Triple Helix Group at Newcastle University Business School: Dr. Marina Ranga, Dr. James Dzisah, Dr. Lucy Lu, Dr. Glenwyn Kemp, and Miss Dessy Irwati. Finally, I wish to express my appreciation to John Goddard, Deputy Vice-Chancellor of Newcastle University, for sponsoring the Triple Helix Group. John has also taken the triple helix on a new mission as guiding principle of the UK's Science Cities project.

July 15, 2007
Nantucket

Introduction

The interaction among university, industry, and government is the key to innovation and growth in a knowledge-based economy. In ancient Mesopotamia, a triple helix water screw, invented to raise water from one level to another, was the basis of a hydraulic system of agricultural innovation that irrigated ordinary farms as well as the Hanging Gardens of Babylon, one of the seven wonders of the ancient world.[1] The triple helix as a physical device is succeeded by university–industry–government interactions that have led to the venture capital firm, the incubator, and the science park. These social inventions are hybrid organizations that embody elements of the triple helix in their DNA.

The university is the generative principle of knowledge-based societies just as government and industry were the primary institutions in industrial society. Industry remains a key actor as the locus of production, government as the source of contractual relations that guarantee stable interactions and exchange. The competitive advantage of the university, over other knowledge-producing institutions, is its students. Their regular entry and graduation continually bring in new ideas, in contrast to the research and development (R & D) units of firms and government laboratories that tend to ossify, lacking the "flow-through of human capital" that is built into the university.

Universities, firms, and governments each "take the role of the other" in triple helix interactions even as they maintain their primary roles and distinct identities. The university takes the role of industry by stimulating the development of new firms from research, introducing "the capitalization of knowledge" as an academic goal. Firms develop training to ever higher levels and share knowledge through joint ventures, acting a bit like universities. Governments act as public venture capitalists while continuing their regulatory activities. In contrast to theories that emphasize the role of government or firms in innovation, the triple helix focuses on the university as a source of entrepreneurship and technology as well as critical inquiry.

Entrepreneurship in the triple helix

Envisioning new initiatives, and drawing together the resources to create them, is no longer limited to a narrow range of organizational, ethnic, or gender actors. Universities and governments act as entrepreneurs, demonstrating that entrepreneurship is not limited to business. Entrepreneurial universities play a key role in the triple helix through technology transfer, incubating new firms, and taking the lead in regional renewal efforts. Some of this entrepreneurial activity is based on expectations that utilization of research will spur new ideas as well as income.[2] New research ideas may arise from practical as well as theoretical sources and vice versa, e.g. hedge funds inspired by options-pricing theory.

Entrepreneurship is a group as well as an individual initiative. In countries such as Sweden where individuals are unlikely to take an entrepreneurial initiative without group support, there is a tradition of collective entrepreneurship. Firm-formation does not begin until a group is constituted and agrees to take action. Indeed, collective entrepreneurship is typical of knowledge-based firms that require both technical and business expertise that is unlikely to reside in a single person. Entrepreneurs may be professors, engineers, or inventors as well as businesspersons. Policy entrepreneurs like Esko Aho, a recent prime minister of Finland who invigorated the Finnish innovation system, may also be recognized.

An entrepreneurial model is spreading to societies that heretofore relied primarily on administrative initiatives. In Africa, entrepreneurial initiatives have emerged as the university has stepped in to solve national technological crises, creating spin-off firms as an unintended consequence. When the telecommunications system broke down in Zambia several years ago, the University of Zambia's Computer Centre extended a campus-based email network across the country. Eventually this initiative was spun off as an independent firm and the experience became the basis for future explicitly entrepreneurial initiatives.

Entrepreneurship has also expanded with the realization that it can be taught to a wide variety of persons. A rapid advance in entrepreneurial education has taken place in Brazil, where it has expanded across the university to the arts and sciences, from the engineering and business schools. Undergraduate students at the Pontifical Catholic University of Rio de Janeiro (PUC), and increasingly in other Brazilian universities, are required to take a basic course in entrepreneurship. Just as every student is expected to be able to write an essay expressing their personal thoughts or craft a scientific paper, utilizing evidence to test hypotheses, the ability to write a business plan, setting forth an objective and a means to test its validity, is held to be an essential element of the undergraduate curriculum at PUC. The Brazilian undergraduate educational model focuses on identifying entrepreneurial talents in students who may have previously lacked awareness of their latent abilities.

Entrepreneurship may also occur in places that do not recognize its relevance. For example, Purchase College's educational program in theater and dance is based on an implicit incubation model as students go through the program, organized into theater and dance troupes, with some of them continuing after graduation. Most students in a class at this liberal-arts college were bewildered when exposed to the concept of the "business plan" by a guest lecturer, Magnus Klofsten, professor of entrepreneurship at Linköping University in Sweden. However, when the class was stopped and restarted with the question "At some time in your life, would you like to establish a new organization, whether a business, school, theater, dance troupe, etc.?", two-thirds of the students stated this as their objective.

Entrepreneurial training should be a part of general education in an era in which formation of new organizations in all aspects of life is increasingly commonplace. Should the capability to write a business plan not be an element of every university graduate's repertoire in an era when many students either will be expected to generate their own employment and/or have as one of their life goals participation in the creation of a new venture? Entrepreneurship and circulation among the institutional spheres of university–industry and government, rather than pursuit of a single path, are becoming the norm. The implications of the triple helix transcend innovation and influence the way we work and interact.

Contents of this book

Chapter 1, "Pathways to the triple helix," presents the contrasting sources of the movement toward a common triple helix model of relatively independent overlapping institutional spheres that foster cooperation for innovation. Chapter 2, "The entrepreneurial university," discusses the transformation of the university and how it has come to play a role in innovation through an extension of the traditional research and teaching mission of academia into a new focus on economic and social development. Chapter 3, "The evolution of the firm," treats the emergence of start-up formats linked to academic research. The triple helix firm comprises organizational and cultural elements drawn from business, academia, and government. Chapter 4, "The optimum role of government," discusses the role of government in innovation, under contrasting conditions in which the state plays either a direct or an indirect role in innovation.

Chapter 5, "Regional innovation," analyzes the transformation of the region from a geographical, cultural, and industrial area to an innovation entity—the triple helix region. A regional infrastructure that has the ability to move from one technology paradigm to another, as the earlier one becomes exhausted, is required. A conceptual framework of knowledge, consensus, and innovation spaces is suggested for thinking about regional development in terms of the interaction among the triple helix actors to fill gaps in a region and enhance its development with discontinuous innovation.

Chapter 6, "Triple helix technopolis," examines the intersection of various organizational mechanisms designed to link the productive sector to academia and their development into a common framework to smooth the path of technology transfer. Chapter 7, "The incubation of innovation," focuses on the evolution of the incubator as a support structure for high-tech start-ups based on academic research and how it has been applied to a broader set of industrial and social problems. Chapter 8, "Reinventing venture capital," analyzes the invention of the venture capital firm as a regional development strategy and its transformation into a financial mechanism. Chapter 9, "The endless transition," argues that the linear model of discontinuous innovation emerging from science has become an assisted linear model, through the creation of a dynamic triple helix ecosystem that fosters economic and social development.

Innovation from the knowledge base

Innovation, the reconfiguration of elements into a more productive combination, takes on a broader meaning in increasingly knowledge-based societies. Formerly the development of new products in firms, innovation also includes the creation of organizational arrangements that enhance the innovative process. Only a small group of specialists in industry and academia were interested in innovation when it was limited to the analysis of product improvement. In recent years the appropriate configuration of relationships between firm-formation, high technology, and economic growth has become a matter of public concern and debate.

As jobs are outsourced, what will be the future engine of economic growth, especially as "high-tech," as well as manufacturing positions, are increasingly relocated to countries with highly skilled persons and lower wages? Is the university losing its traditional role and independence as it becomes more closely involved with, and presumably subordinate to, industry and government; or is it attaining a higher level of status and influence in society, thereby enhancing its independence, as it takes on a more central role in society through its contribution to innovation?

And, of course, not all agree that the university should play an entrepreneurial role. Many academics believe that the university best fulfills its mission by limiting itself to education and research, eschewing a broader role in economic and social development. According to this view, the university best fulfills the third mission by fulfilling the first two.[3] Nevertheless, there is increasing interest in pursuing the practical implications of research even among those academics who were most skeptical about the capitalization of knowledge.[4]

A series of research projects on innovation mechanisms, conducted from the early 1980s, mostly sponsored by the US National Science Foundation, provide the empirical base for this volume. These studies have been supplemented by visits and research projects in various countries typically sponsored by universities, think tanks, and regional and national development agencies that allowed me to make this analysis comparative. The Center for Business and Policy Studies in Stockholm sponsored the original version of this manuscript, published in Swedish. My current academic home, the Newcastle University Business School, is the base for a research program extending analyses of the triple helix to the European Union and beyond.

There is increasing awareness that a knowledge-based society operates according to a different set of dynamics than an industrial society focused on manufacturing tangible goods. Knowledge-based economies are more tightly linked to sources of new knowledge; they are also subject to continuous transformation instead of being rooted in stable arrangements. Fostering a continuous process of firm-formation based on advanced technologics, oftcn university-originated, moves to the heart of innovation strategy. This volume extrapolates nascent trends into a vision of the seminal role of the university in a knowledge-based society.

1 Pathways to the triple helix

Introduction

Scientific roles are in flux with the elimination of clear dividing lines between science and business. Scientists in a late 1970s California solar electricity start-up did not fit previous sociological definitions of academic or industrial scientist. These physicists were "entrepreneurial scientists"[1] who participated in decision-making as backers of the firm, with funds earned from stock options in the semiconductor industry. They were not interested in publication,[2] as their goal was patents, nor did they suffer the "role strain" of corporate scientists making the transition from academia, torn between their allegiances.[3] Moreover, academic scientists, doing start-ups from their research, are on both sides of the university–industry relationship.

University–industry relations also often had a third partner. Studies by Professor Rosalba Casas and members of her research group at the National Autonomous University of Mexico (UNAM) showed that university and industry in Mexico primarily interact through their links to government; thus government's role was highlighted. In the US, where government's role is often suppressed, government has played a key role in setting the stage for university–industry interactions through changes in the patent law and through provision of "public venture capital" for start-ups in the form of research grants. A triple helix of university–industry–government interactions was the result of these trends.

The triple helix was generated from an analysis of government's relation to university and industry in different societies and its various roles in innovation.[4] The growth of new firms from academic research and the location of science-based industry adjacent to universities is a manifestation of triple helix relations in knowledge-based societies. Innovation increasingly takes form in triple helix relations and the new types of innovation actors that are invented through these interactions include incubators, science parks, and venture capital firms. In the following, we outline the origin and development of the triple helix model of innovation.

Triple helix innovation

Innovation takes on a new meaning as the spirals of the triple helix intertwine. Even in its original sense of product development, innovation is no longer only the special province of industry. Knowledge-producing institutions have become more important to innovation as knowledge becomes an increasingly significant element in new product development. This expansion of the concept of innovation makes university and government significant actors in the innovation process, collaboratively as well as individually.

The triple helix is a platform for "institution formation," the creation of new organizational formats to promote innovation, as a synthesis of elements of the triple helix. The triple helix captures this transformation of roles and relationships as intertwined spirals with different relations to each other. In a laissez-faire triple helix regime, industry is the driving force, with the other two spirals as ancillary supporting structures; in a statist regime government plays the lead role, driving academia and industry. Spirals are rarely equal; one usually serves as a motive force, the innovation organizer (IO) around which the others rotate. The institution that acts as the core spiral changes over time as one spiral replaces the other as the driving force in a triple helix configuration.

Triple helix impetus

A triple helix regime typically begins as university, industry, and government enter into a reciprocal relationship with each other in which each attempts to enhance the performance of the other. Most such initiatives take place at the regional level, where specific contexts of industrial clusters, academic development, and presence or lack or governing authority influence the development of the triple helix.

The first step toward a triple helix is usually collaboration among the institutional spheres most involved with innovation, taking place through their traditional roles. For example, universities, firms, and governments in a region may participate in discussions to enhance a local economy, develop a regional growth agreement, or establish a technology council. As a result municipalities may agree to speed up building-permitting processes for new plant construction, universities may undertake to train more students in an area relevant to the local economy and firms may negotiate new supplier relationships with each other as an incipient cluster. At this initial level of the triple helix, the three strands typically begin to interact in order to improve the local economy by enhancing the performance of existing industry.

The triple helix changes its spin as production of new knowledge and technology becomes more important. At this level of the triple helix, enhancement of the performance of the university and other knowledge-producing institutions often becomes the key issue as part of a strategy to renew an older economy or create new economic activity on the basis of intellectual capital in one form or another, ranging from formal R & D in government, university, and industrial laboratories to tacit knowledge emanating from existing industries.

As a new overlay of knowledge infuses existing industry and as various combinations of new and old knowledge become the basis for firm-formation, the university and other knowledge-producing institutions replace industry as the core spiral. Government and industry may then become involved in supporting academic development. The establishment of a research center, speeding up academic research production, is a typical strategy. The university gains additional resources from industry and government to enhance the performance of research, one of its traditional functions.

Taking the role of the other

The next step to development of the triple helix is internal transformation of the institutions in which, in addition to performing its traditional tasks, each "takes the role of the other." A second level of innovation in innovation arises as the triple helix actors take on new tasks. If a function is already performed by an institution that has it as its core competency, the utility of another institution taking it on as a secondary activity is the innovative contribution it may make to the performance of this role.

In addition to instigating new activities, "taking the role of the other" contributes to the traditional missions, as when participation in the capitalization of knowledge leads to the development of new academic research and educational programs. Each institutional sphere is thus more likely to become a creative source of innovation and to support the emergence of creativity that arises in other spirals. Going beyond traditional missions, universities were the source of the venture capital and incubation movements that were enhanced by the support of industry and government.

As they take the role of the other, each institution maintains its primary role and distinct identity. The fundamental role of the university as an institution for the preservation and transmission of knowledge remains its core mission. Thus universities continue their special mission of socialization of youth and dissemination of knowledge even as they take on some business and governance functions. Similarly, government is the ultimate guarantor of societal rules of the game and industry is the primary source of productive activities. Thus industry continues to produce goods and services and also does research, but increasingly provides training at higher levels, reflected in the fact that many companies now have their own "universities," at least in their special area of expertise. Government is responsible for providing the rules of the game but also makes available venture capital to help start new enterprises.

From bilateral to trilateral interactions

Bilateral interactions among university–government, university–industry and government–industry increase through role-taking. Even as the core identity of each institution is maintained, it is enhanced in new ways through relationships with other spheres. Thus the university trains organizations in incubators as well as individuals in classrooms. Moreover, as the university engages in technology transfer it becomes a source of new product development, which is, of course, a traditional industrial function. The entrepreneurial university, exemplified by the Massachusetts Institute of Technology (MIT), participates in the economic and social development of its region. Entrepreneurship as an academic mission is integrated with teaching and research. As the university assumes an entrepreneurial role internally, it naturally also becomes more closely involved with industry, especially since there is not such a great distance between the institutional spheres.

At MIT, the classic entrepreneurial university, involvement with industry occurred through a series of organizational innovations that legitimated the interaction between the two spheres.[5] This included the invention of the one-fifth rule regulating consultation as the resolution of a decade-long controversy. The legal concept of the contract was utilized to formalize hitherto informal university–industry ties. The development of organizational capacities to interact with industry, through a liaison office to identify appropriate industrial partners, was a next step. This was followed by the utilization of intermediary organizations to carry out business with industry, such as the sale of intellectual property rights in the 1920s and 1930s that the university was not yet prepared to conduct on its own. In the US, university–government relations were often constructed from the models initially developed for relations with industry; in other societies the movement has been in the opposite direction.

The growth of university–government relations was intertwined with the formation of national identity in Germany in the early 19th century, with the so-called Humboldtian academic model integrating teaching and research. Apart from the land grant tradition, strong university–government relations in the US emerged from the World War II military research projects. These were undertaken at the behest of academic scientists who saw, on the one hand, the potential to develop advanced weaponry through the application of science to military problems (radar) and, on the other, the ultimate outcome of theoretical advance (the atomic bomb). University–government relations transcended the wartime emergency as academics realized that theoretical advance could arise from problem-oriented research as well as vice versa.

As bilateral interactions take place, they tend to bring in the third element of the triple helix to solve problems and meet new needs. It is a global phenomenon that involves "learning by borrowing," importing and adapting organizational models from abroad, as well as independent invention. For example, the incubator concept that had been imported from the US to Brazil was reinvented and made more relevant to local circumstances than the US academic model focused on high-tech firm-formation based upon academic research. Starting from an academic base of limited high-tech capacity, Brazilians soon transformed the incubator into a broader model to address issues of development and poverty.

Having realized that the essential purpose of an incubator was to teach a group of people to act as an organization, as an extension of the classic educational mission of the university as well as an expression of its new economic and social development remit, the model was applied to a variety of purposes within and without academia. Industrial associations entered the field, creating incubators to expand traditional clusters. Municipalities also established incubators as a job creation strategy. A nongovernmental organization (NGO), in collaboration with a university high-tech incubator, applied the model to organize cooperatives, training poor people from the *favelas* to run their own organizations and create jobs for themselves. An association of incubators, ANPROTEC, brought the different incubator types and their supporters together in a common framework.

The incubator movement in Brazil originated in the universities in the face of considerable skepticism toward introducing a support structure to found new technology firms from academic research, expressed as charges of "privatization of the university." The incubator was legitimized when a municipal government took an interest and funded a building for an early incubator, allowing the project to move from temporary quarters, precipitating acceptance as an official unit.

Expansion and rapid growth of a university initiative to create incubator facilities took place as industrial associations and various levels of government became involved. Support from industry associations and state governments extended the concept from high-technology firms to raising the level of technology in existing firms. The critique of incubation abated as university technology transfer organizations also established incubators to train low-income persons to organize cooperatives. A national government initiative then extended this project to universities across the country.

As the number of sources and levels of initiative increase among the triple helix actors, a meta-innovation system is created. The premise for the growth of such a dynamic is an active civil society in which initiatives are encouraged from various parts of society. The possibility of individuals and groups to freely organize, debate, and take initiatives is the basis for a triple helix including bottom-up as well as top-down initiatives.

A triple helix embedded in a flourishing civil society encourages the emergence of diverse sources of innovation. Creating an organization or network, representing different interests, in order to build support for a regional focus is a key element in such a strategy. Individuals, typically from the triple helix spheres, come together to brainstorm ideas, formulate initiatives and seek out resources to promote regional development initiatives. Examples include the Pittsburgh High-tech Council, the Niteroi Technopole in Brazil, the Knowledge Circle of Amsterdam and Joint Venture Silicon Valley in San Jose, California. The prototypical instance was the New England Council, founded during the 1920s, bringing together industrial, academic, and governmental leadership to address the region's long-term economic decline.

Toward the triple helix by different routes

The path to the triple helix begins from two opposing standpoints: a statist model of government controlling academia and industry (Figure 1.1), and a laissez-faire model with industry, academia, and government separate and apart from each other, interacting only modestly across strong boundaries (Figure 1.2). From both of these standpoints there is, on the one hand, movement toward greater independence of university and industry from the state and, on the other, greater interdependence of these institutional spheres. Interaction among the institutional spheres of university, industry, and government, playing both their own traditional roles and each other's, in various combinations, is a stimulant to organizational creativity. New organizational innovations especially arise from interactions among the three helices (Figure 1.3). The common triple helix format supersedes variation in national innovation systems.

Our purpose here is to elucidate the transition to a triad of equal and overlapping institutional spheres. Double helices, lacking a third mediating element, tend toward conflictual relations.[6] The question of the appropriate balance between industry and government, including the role of labor and capital in society, is expressed in theories and social movements that promote socialism or capitalism. A struggle between proponents

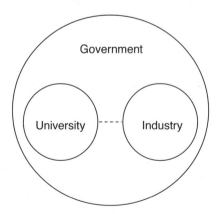

Figure 1.1 The statist model.

of these two basic societal formats has ensued since the inception and growth of the modern state and industry, from the 18th century.[7] Nevertheless, there is a basic commonality of laissez-faire and statist regimes despite apparently divergent formats. This structural similarity is exemplified by the interchangeability of government and industry in leading roles in various theories of reform capitalism and market socialism.

Statist and laissez-faire regimes, the traditional competing models of social organization in modern societies, represent reverse sides of the government–industry coin. Statist societies emphasize the coordinating role of government while laissez-faire societies focus on the productive force of industry as the prime mover of economic and social development. Both formats emphasize the primacy of these two institutional spheres, albeit in drastically different proportions. Thus strong and weak roles for government and industry respectively are the defining characteristics of statist regimes while the reverse relationship is the basis of laissez-faire societies.

Statist society

In some countries, government is the dominant institutional sphere. Industry and the university are subordinate parts of the state. When relationships are organized among the institutional spheres, government plays the coordinating role. In this model, government is expected to take the lead in developing projects and providing the resources for new initiatives.

Industry and academia are seen to be relatively weak institutional spheres that require strong guidance, if not control. The former Soviet Union, France, and many Latin American countries exemplify the statist model of societal organization.

The statist model relies on specialized organizations linked hierarchically by central government. Translated into science and technology policy,

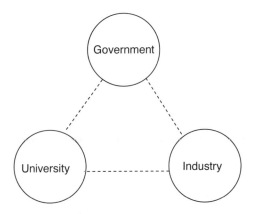

Figure 1.2 The laissez-faire model.

the statist model is characterized by specialized basic and applied research institutes, including sectoral units for particular industries. Universities are largely teaching institutions, distant from industry. A central planning agency was a key feature of the Soviet version of the statist model. A decision was required from the central planning agency to arrange implementation of institute research. Waiting on such a decision often became a block to technology transfer since the firms and the institutes could not arrange the matter directly, at least not through formal channels.

In the 1960s the Argentinian physicist Jorge Sabato set forth a "triangular" science and technology policy model, applying the statist model to a developing country, arguing that only government had the ability and resources to take the lead in coordinating the other institutional spheres to create science-based industry. In Brazil, during the era of the military regime, the federal government's science and technology policies of the 1970s and early 1980s implicitly attempted to realize Sabato's vision. Large-scale projects were funded by government to support the creation of new technological industries such as aircraft, computers, and electronics. The projects typically included funds to raise the level of academic research to support these technology development programs. A side effect was increased local training of graduate students to work in the projects.

The role of government increases in all countries in times of national emergency. The US, for example, reorganized itself on a statist basis during the two world wars, placing industry and university in the service of the state. The Manhattan Project to develop the atomic bomb during World War II concentrated scientific and industrial resources at a few key locations, under military control, to accomplish this goal. The recurrent calls for a Manhattan-type project to address such diverse problems as cancer and poverty suggest the attraction of the statist model even in countries with a laissez-faire ideology. Indeed, the statist model can produce great results, with good leadership, a clear objective, and commitment of significant resources.

The statist model often carries with it the objective that the country should develop its technological industry separately from what is happening in the rest of the world. In Europe this model can be seen in terms of companies that are expected to be the dominant national leader in a particular field, with the government supporting those companies, such as the Bull computer company in France. In this configuration the role of the university is primarily seen as one of providing trained persons to work in the other spheres. It may conduct research but it is not expected to play a role in the creation of new enterprises.

Even in France, the classic statist regime, many of these expectations have changed in recent years.[8] Efforts have been made to decentralize elite knowledge-producing institutions from Paris in order to create other alternative sources of initiative. Although not yet at the level of the German *Länder* or the American state government, a new level of regional government gains resources and is able to take its own initiatives. Start-up firms, initially offshoots of military programs, begin to take on a life of their own.

Change in statist societies is impelled by the need to speed up the innovation system by introducing new sources of initiative. Bureaucratic coordination concentrates initiative at the top and tends to suppress ideas that arise from below. Lateral informal relations across the spheres partially override formal top-down procedures. However, such working around the system is typically confined to relatively limited initiatives. When there is a need to undertake larger scale initiatives, the way is often blocked, outside of the military and space spheres that were given extraordinary priorities in the former Soviet Union.

Laissez-faire society

Another starting point for the triple helix model is separation among institutional spheres. Ideology and reality often diverge, with the spheres operating more closely together than expected. In the US, for example, skepticism of government often obscures the emergence of the triple helix. In reality the institutional spheres are closer together than is commonly held, but accepted US belief is the model of government, industry, and academia operating in their own areas without close connections.

In this model, the university is a provider of basic research and trained persons. Its role in connection with industry is to supply knowledge, mainly in the form of publications and graduates who bring tacit knowledge with them to their new jobs. It is up to industry to find useful knowledge from the universities without expectation of much assistance. Industry is also expected to operate on its own, with firms linked to each other by the market relationships of buying and selling. There is expected to be intense competition among firms, with collaboration forbidden.

Corporations were forbidden by law to cooperate and collaborate with each other because it was expected that if they did communicate extensively the first thing that they were likely to do would be to form a cartel and set prices of products. Thus, for the most part, companies were discouraged from interacting, except through meetings of associations where people could get together according to their professional specialization. Firms in an industry were thus expected to operate independently from each other both in their R & D and in product development.

As international industrial competition became greater, it was argued that some of these rules would have to be changed. In the 1970s, in the US, increased international competition from Japan led to a rethinking of appropriate relationships among companies in peacetime circumstances. The antitrust rules were changed to allow companies to do pre-competitive research and then to allow joint product development. Industry was encouraged to restructure according to the framework of strategic alliances among different companies. A concept of competition was invented to denote that companies should not only compete, but should cooperate and collaborate.

In the laissez-faire model the role of government is expected to be limited to clear cases of so-called "market failure," when economic impetuses by themselves do not call an activity into existence. Government is expected to play a limited role of regulation or of buying products but not necessarily in the military area where there is much closer linkage. For example, the US military economy operates according to the statist model, through top-down direction by government, with industry and universities playing a significant role within that coordination.[9]

Government is expected to play a larger civilian role only when an activity cannot be provided by the market. No one is prepared to offer the function for sale or perform it; therefore it must be provided by government. It is on the basis of this argument of market failure that it is agreed that the government may provide funds to the university to support research because the market will not meet that need. Since it would not take place otherwise, it is accepted that there is a limited role for government.

There is expected to be only limited interaction between university, industry, and government in a laissez-faire regime. When there are interactions and interrelationships among the spheres, they are expected to take place across strongly defended boundaries and preferably through an intermediary. For example, for many years before US universities became directly involved in patenting research there was an organization called the Research Corporation, an independent not-for-profit organization

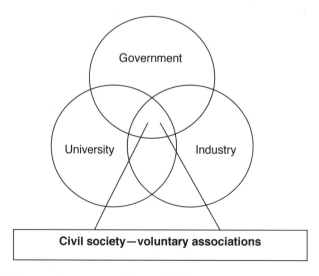

Figure 1.3 The social structure of the triple helix.

between the universities and industry that found research in universities that could be patented and then arranged for its transfer to a company that found it of interest. Thus industry and university did not relate directly but through an intermediary organization. Basically, it was argued that it was not appropriate for them to be in direct contact with each other. Nevertheless, if they needed to be in contact, it should be through someone else playing an intermediary role. Thus to the extent that there were relationships, they tended to occur at arm's length.

Attentions to boundary maintenance, separate spheres, distinct institutional roles, and firms as the locus of economic activity characterize laissez-faire society. Concern for boundaries is typically part of a larger complex of ideas and beliefs related to the purity of institutional spheres. Functions and spheres are believed to be related on a one-to-one basis, i.e. industry = production; government = regulation; university = basic research.[10] Expansion or crossover of functions from one sphere to another is *ipso facto* evidence of decline, for some, while for others it is a sign of organizational and individual creativity.

Behind a laissez-faire façade, individualistic expressions such as the "individual investigator" denoting the lead researcher in the university actually represent research groups that operate as "quasi-firms," the virtual small-business format in which academic science typically takes place. An extension of government research funding programs, in the guise of mere exploration of the practical implications of their research, provides the equivalent of venture capital for scientific entrepreneurs to create actual firms. California Proposition 71, an implicit triple helix initiative, provides 3 billion dollars for stem cell R & D, utilizing debt-funding mechanisms such as bond issues to provide grants to university research groups and biotechnology start-ups. The expectation is that a virtuous circle will be created, with intellectual property and equity in firms generated to pay off the public debt incurred.

Nevertheless, significant ethical issues develop at the interface, especially as individuals perform dual roles. Conflicts of interest may arise from individuals, holding positions in more than one organization, as in the California program to fund university research groups and biotechnology firms. An individual's financial interest and even scientific judgment may be affected by holding two positions. On the other hand, holding these multiple standpoints facilitates technology transfer and scientific creativity. For example, Newcastle University has introduced a professors-of-practice (PoP) scheme to recruit serial entrepreneurs to its faculties. The ideal candidate is expected to be a PhD with industrial experience, for example a high-tech-firm entrepreneur who has developed ideas for advanced technology that are more appropriate to research in a university than in a firm environment.

Conflict of interest is transmuted into confluence of interest in this model. A 50-percent appointment allows the PoP to establish a research group and seek funds for its support while maintaining a serious involvement in his or her firm. Based on the premise that knowledge may be theoretical and applied at one and the same time, and with appropriate guidelines and good will, such a "dual life" person is expected to provide a role model for regular professors whose inventions may have entrepreneurial potential as well as infuse the university with new research ideas from industrial practice.

Resolving conflicts of interest and apparent conflicts is a continuous balancing act that must take into account retaining the advantages arising from confluences of interest that are an outcome of individual involvement in two or more spheres. Strategies for dealing with conflicts include publicly stating dual affiliations and removing oneself from decision-making when two competing organizations are involved. However, necessary expertise can be lost if this principle is carried too far, as journal editors have discovered in allowing academics with connections to biotech firms to review contributions, despite their commercial involvement. With commercial involvement the norm in this academic area, there would otherwise be a paucity of reviewers.

The emergence of conflict-of-interest issues may also be taken as a positive sign of organizational flux and creativity in rigid organizational structures. As has been succinctly noted, "no conflict, no interest." The university enhances itself and its role in society as it integrates its new mission of contributing to economic and social development into a productive relationship with research and teaching, each inspiring the other, belying pessimistic theses of academic decline.[11] Triple helix field theory elucidates these roles and relationships.[12]

Triple helix field theory[13]

Triple helix field theory depicts helices with an internal core and external field space (Figure 1.4). The model helps explain why the three spheres keep a relatively independent and distinct status, shows where interactions take place, and explains why a dynamic triple helix can be formed with gradations between independence and interdependence, conflict and confluence of interest. Conversely, the model can be used to help identify when a sphere is in danger of losing its identity.

The university can play industry's role, in assisting firm-formation and technology transfer, but not as a true enterprise. The same holds for industry and government. Industry may form university-like teaching and research entities, but it is unlikely to stray too far from its core mission. This explains the decline and even disappearance of these auxiliary enterprises in economic downturns.

An institutional sphere may lose its distinct character if it cannot maintain its relative independence. For example, an academically oriented start-up may focus too exclusively on research and lose its way to the

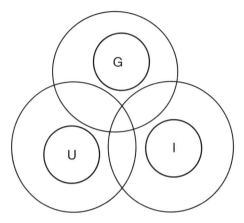

Figure 1.4 Triple helix field interaction model.

market. It is also very difficult for highly dependent spheres to interact in the external field space, since the confusion of functions or roles inevitably results in a disordered system. This explains why universities place their endowment funds in separate entities that operate on financial principles, separate from the academic enterprise.

On the other hand, technology transfer has been seen to be an extension of the academic research and teaching task and thus has been retained within the academic core. Taking the role of the other does not necessarily imply loss of a sphere's core identity—the notion that taking even the smallest step may result in an irrevocable transformation. Rather it may be an indicator of institutional change and renovation. The taking on of a new mission or role may enhance, as well as detract from, old ones. A careful balancing and willingness to experiment is the apparently contradictory, yet only healthy, prescription.

When a field exists with energy around it, the field can act upon its surroundings. In an electric field, for example, the action on charges put in a field space is represented by the force of the electric field. The endured force per unit charge is defined as the intensity of the electric field, describing the strong or weak degree to which the field influences the charge. Thus intensity of field is introduced, indicating the degree to which helices promote innovation activities. If E represents the total field intensity, and Eu, Ei, and Eg respectively represent the intensity of university, industry, and government actions, then E = f (Eu, Ei, and Eg) the result of the interaction (Figure 1.5).[14]

Field theory illustrates the importance of limiting the transformation from laissez-faire to overlapping spheres or of not too sharply reducing a statist model, in order to retain each sphere's independence while facilitating interaction. For example, if government is too strong, then a

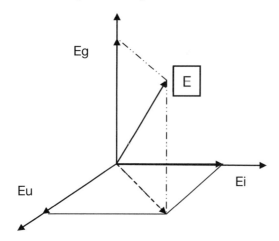

Figure 1.5 Synthetic interaction of triple helix.

statist model might be formed. If the interactions among the three helices are too weak, there is not enough force to integrate them, leading to a laissez-faire situation.

Analyzing lost or weak factors, "gaps," and filling them helps create balanced triple helices. A regional innovation organizer (RIO) and regional innovation initiator (RII) exercise different yet related gap-filling capabilities. A RIO provides convening capabilities while an RII must have sufficient prestige and authority to aggregate resources and initiate an enterprise.

The governors of New England convened regional academic, industrial, and governmental leadership in a series of meetings from the late 1920s, but it was Karl Compton, the president of MIT, who eventually catalyzed ideas for science-based firm-formation and mobilized regional leadership to act. Conversely, when the New York Academy of Sciences convened a series of meetings of representatives of university, industry, and government to support knowledge-based economic development in the mid-1990s, it was unable to make the transition from RIO to RII and to take discussion into action.

Triple helix circulation

Knowledge capitalization has various sources in industry, universities, and government institutes. When knowledge is transformed into capital, persons from any originating organization may be potential entrepreneurs and founders of firms. A triple helix in which each strand may relate to the other two can be expected to develop an "overlay of communications, networks, and organizations among the helices."[15] Figure 1.6 reflects the

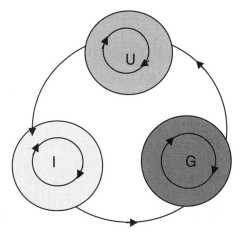

Figure 1.6 Circulation of individuals in the triple helix.

spirally-developing triple helix: a synthesis of evolution in the vertical axis and circulation in the horizontal.

Triple helix field interaction sheds light on why there is circulation, but it does not show what factors participate in it and how it works. Figure 1.6 depicts a triple helix circulation that occurs on "macro and micro" levels. Macro circulations move among the helices, while micro circulations take place within a particular helix. The former create collaboration policies, projects, and networks while the latter consist of the outputs of individual helices.

Lateral social mobility, introduction of expertise from one social sphere to another, can stimulate hybridization, invention, and innovation of new social formats. Horizontal circulation is thus more likely to have a radicalizing effect than vertical circulation with its inherent conservative bias. Vertical circulation occurs through upward and downward movement of individuals within an institutional sphere, typically through recruitment of new persons of talent from lower strata, revivifying an elite.[16]

The university is the quintessential institution designed to promote lateral circulation through its educational function. Students arrive from families that are connected to different social spheres and some move on to new spheres, rather than reproducing old ones. Recently, lateral movement has also taken place at the upper levels of the university, drawing in administrators and teachers, with skills gained in other social spheres and sending out professors to government and industry, with expertise needed in those institutions.

The movement across helices is sometimes viewed as creating conflicts of interest due to too close association of roles in different spheres. But the bright side is institutional cross-fertilization, whereby each helix is infused with new ideas and perspectives from the others through the circulation of individuals. The emergence of conflicts of interest, until now viewed solely for their negative implications, may also be an augur of the invention of innovative roles and new organizational designs, especially ones that cross-cut traditional spheres.

Circulation of individuals

Personnel circulation around the triple helix has been called a "revolving door." The American sociologist C. Wright Mills (1958) strongly criticized this phenomenon as resulting in corporate dominance of government and untoward military influence in industry.[17] People flow may also introduce ideas from one sphere to another, sparking collaborative projects and promoting cross-institutional understanding. Indeed, lack of circulation of elites may be a cause of blocked development in countries whose leadership has nowhere to go once they complete their term in office.

At least three types of circulation can be identified:

1   *Unidirectional or permanent movement from one sphere to another.* On the university–industry interface, high-tech-firm entrepreneurs who were university professors exemplify the flow from university to industry, e.g. A. Bose moved from MIT to his acoustical firm while retaining a tie as adjunct professor. Reversely, from industry to university, the archetypal figure is the coinventor of the transistor, William Bradford Shockley, who entered Stanford University as a faculty member from industry in 1963.

2   *Dual life, or holding simultaneous significant positions in two spheres, such as a half-time position in industry and a professorship.* Provost Terman invited Carl Djerassi, research director of the Syntex pharmaceutical firm, to be a chemistry professor at Stanford as part of the strategy of building steeples of excellence in focused fields with significant intellectual and commercial potential, in this instance steroid chemistry. Djerassi brought the firm's R & D operation with him to Palo Alto from Mexico City and continued as research director as part of his arrangement with Stanford.[18]

3   *Alternation, or significant successive periods of time in more than one sphere.* Stanford professor William Perry, for example, after a significant business career and half-time professorship, served as secretary of defense and then returned to the university on a full-time basis.

Information circulation: innovation networks

Collaboration is premised on information communication that, in the information technology (IT) era, increasingly occurs through networks at various levels, from local to international. Some information networks are designed to announce government policies and funding sources, cutting-edge research results from universities and their implications for new technologies and industries; collaboration needs from industry. Others are also designed to support innovative regions. For example, Oresund, the cross-border region linked by a bridge between Copenhagen and Malmö, is both an information communication network between Denmark and Sweden and an innovative region.[19]

Output circulation: reciprocity among actors

Reciprocity among actors and equality of contribution to innovation are further crucial factors. If there is a negative imbalance in contributions, a gap might appear in innovation; conversely a positive imbalance might stimulate other actors to increase their efforts. For example, the products of start-up firms in the nascent semiconductor industry in California initially caught the attention of the Department of Defense and NASA as a means to miniaturize equipment. The civilian expansion of that industry followed—scientific research results by scientists such as Shockley were recognized by industry, e.g. the potential of solid-state physics to create better telephone switching devices.

World War II was a key inflection point, transforming university–government relations. Prior to the war, most academic scientists were located in teaching universities, "where they had no opportunity to do research . . . relocated by the war, they suddenly found themselves in well-equipped laboratories and moved rapidly to apply their pent up energies and talents to the R & D needed for the war effort."[20] Exemplified by Vannevar Bush, academics initiated policies for wartime mobilization of scientific talent and sought to attain both civilian and military objectives after the war.[21]

University faculties have accepted funding and policies to support entrepreneurial activities from government since World War II, scaling up research in key fields such as computer science.[22] The confluence of these forces transformed relatively modest university-originated regional innovation dynamics in Boston and northern California into economic dynamos. Silicon Valley has since metamorphosed into a global innovation organizer, importing start-ups and exporting future firm-founders to other regions world-wide in the Silicon Valley diaspora.

Nonlinear innovation

Innovation increasingly combines market and scientific orientations. In the face of skepticism from the military sponsors of artificial-intelligence research in the mid-1970s, the head of the computing office in the Defense Advanced Research Program (DARPA) of the US Defense Department concluded that it would be to the mutual advantage of all for the academic

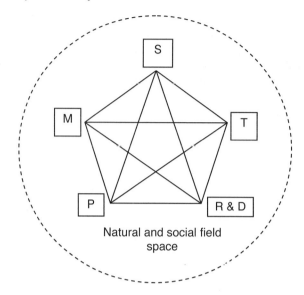

Figure 1.7 Non-linear and netlike pentagonal model of technological innovation.

researchers to take an interest in their sponsors, practical problems: "the shift will give the university research groups an engineering arm, a marketplace, customers, users. [That] integration will strengthen the basic work because there will be more feedback from real tests of the big new ideas."[23] The author of this statement, a psychologist involved in the early development of computer science as an academic discipline, the redoubtable J. C. R. Licklider of Internet origin fame, joined DARPA from MIT, after a stint at Bolt, Beranek, and Newman (BBN),[24] a consulting and research firm.[25]

Figure 1.7 describes a nonlinear and netlike innovation model that may begin from different starting points among science, engineering, R & D, production, and marketing activity. For example, John Bardeen, one of the inventors of the transistor, "believed it made sense to look first at the technological base and then work on developing the corresponding science," rather than the other way around, "finding something in science and then looking around for applications."[26] Thus an innovation may take place in the order of market → technology → science → technology → R & D → production → marketing, or marketing → technology → science → R & D → production → marketing, or any other way.

Conclusion: triple helix and classical social theory

Georg Simmel's, Karl Marx's, and Max Weber's ideas inform the triple helix of interconnected and partially autonomous institutional spheres.

Simmel's analysis of triadic relationships is given an institutional cast: university, industry, and government each may act as a *tertius gaudens* instigating innovation.[27] An interaction of two parties may become stuck, either in hyper-agreement (love) or in excessive conflict, resulting in divorce. A third factor allows a dispassionate element to be introduced into the relationship, mediating, and potentially reducing, the tendency to over-identification on the one hand and escalation of divisiveness on the other.

Marx laid the groundwork for a theory of differentiated social spheres by analyzing the separation of a capitalistic economy from the feudal social relations of medieval society. The shift from the household economy depicted by Aristotle, with production moved from home to factory and work separated from family life, was a key event.[28] Marx also posited science as a source of the future economy, based on a single crucial instance: William Henry Perkin's research on dyestuffs in England developed into an industry in Germany.

The growth of science-based technology, from the 17th century, intersecting with the emergence of independent institutional spheres in the 18th century, founded a new dynamics of innovation. These two dimensions came together in the creation of the research university in the 19th century, incorporating experimental science. The teaching laboratory was invented, scaling up the integration of research and teaching, including research with practical implications, as the university gained autonomy from other social spheres.[29] These twin developments augured the transition from a society based on vertical stratification in the premodern era to one increasingly based on horizontal relationships among institutional spheres.

The vertical hierarchies of the preindustrial and industrial eras—the first based on tradition, the second on expertise—are gradually superseded in the transition from an industrial to a knowledge-based society. A renovation in social relations occurs comparable to the one that took place during the transition to industrial society. The primary factor in each of these transformations is the role of knowledge in society. In feudal society, the most important knowledge was the lore of tradition, the taken-for-granted relationships of superiors and inferiors in society and the obligations that each owed to the other, whereas in industrial society it was the erudition of bureaucracy, how to carry out specific tasks under supervision, the understanding of the basis of willingness to accept orders from above, on the one hand, and the capacity of management to give relevant instructions, on the other.[30]

Three independent dimensions—economics, politics, and status (belief in the reality of social differences based on any criteria)—coexist in a relationship of mutual causation. Political power generates economic wealth and the ability to live off politics, while ideas may be translated into economic and political power. In addition to the accumulation of technological forces, ethical ideas associated with Protestantism were an impetus to the rapid development of economic activity in the West.[31] Other bases for innovation and societal transformation have since been identified. The following chapter discusses the rise of the entrepreneurial university to become the lead institution in the triple helix.

2 The entrepreneurial university

It is important for a medical university to be surrounded by an adequate infrastructure in the form of companies that create applications for research, so that such research may benefit the public. The reverse is also important: the university must respond to commercial issues and utilize commercial expertise.[1]

Introduction

The "capitalization of knowledge" is the heart of a new mission for the university, linking universities to users of knowledge more tightly and establishing the university as an economic actor in its own right. An entrepreneurial university rests on four pillars:

1. academic leadership able to formulate and implement a strategic vision;
2. legal control over academic resources, including physical property such as university buildings and intellectual property emanating from research;
3. organizational capacity to transfer technology through patenting, licensing, and incubation; and
4. an entrepreneurial ethos among administrators, faculty, and students.

Transcending the development of significant research strengths, the entrepreneurial university mines research findings for their technological potential and translates them into use. The university is a natural incubator, providing a support structure for teachers and students to initiate new ventures. Time and space, physical and social, is available to provide the groundwork for "new ventures," whether political, intellectual, or commercial, that are exportable across highly permeable boundaries. The university is also a seedbed for new scientific fields and new industrial sectors, each cross-fertilizing the other. Biotechnology is the recent prime example of this phenomenon as pharmacology was in the 17th century.

Beyond these "natural" entrepreneurial characteristics, an explicitly entrepreneurial university takes the lead in putting knowledge to use and in broadening the input into the creation of academic knowledge. The university must identify the areas of research and teaching that it will focus on to create "steeples of excellence" in order to attract significant support and external funds. An entrepreneurial university also has the capacity to take in and address problems and needs from the larger society, making them the basis of new research projects and intellectual paradigms, creating a virtuous circle with internal intellectual development. This chapter discusses the transition from the research to the entrepreneurial university.

The entrepreneurial university

The transformation of the university into a recognized source of technology, as well as of human resources and knowledge, has created other capabilities to formally transfer technologies than sole reliance on informal ties. In addition to providing new ideas to existing firms, universities are utilizing their research and teaching capabilities in advanced areas of science and technology to form new firms. Universities have also extended their teaching capabilities from educating individuals to shaping organizations in entrepreneurial education and incubation programs. The capitalization of knowledge changes the way that scientists view the results of their research. As the university becomes involved in technology transfer and firm-formation, it attains a new entrepreneurial identity.

The development of an entrepreneurial culture encourages faculty to look at their research results for their commercial as well as their intellectual potential. A technology transfer office, with a mandate to seek out commercializable technology from research and to market it to firms, educates faculty to take an interest in the utilization of their research when an entrepreneurial attitude is weak or non-existent. A culture of entrepreneurship may arise from having to seek external funds in order to conduct research. Alternatively, entrepreneurial attitudes and abilities may be formed in training programs purpose-built to achieve this objective. Scientists who want to achieve recognition from original results also see that their research can have commercial implications. They may participate in the rewards that can be generated, without the two objectives interfering with each other.

The academic enterprise is transformed in parallel with the transition to a knowledge-based economy—sometimes leading it, other times lagging behind. The production of scientific knowledge has become an economic as well as an epistemological enterprise even as the economy increasingly operates on a knowledge-resource base.[2] For the most part, this growth of science-related technologies has remained, "outside the framework of economic models"[3] even as the institutional spheres of science, economy, university, and industry, which were hitherto relatively separate and distinct, have become inextricably intertwined, often through governmental initiatives. Expectations that multinational firms or so-called national champions will be central economic actors in the future are receding. Rather, the key economic actor is increasingly expected to be a cluster of firms emanating from or at least closely associated with a university or other knowledge-producing institution.

The entrepreneurial university as driver of the triple helix

The entrepreneurial university is an academic institution that is under the control of neither government nor industry. Indeed, as the university increases its entrepreneurial activities in relation to commercialization of research, existing industry may view the university as a competitor as well as partner, likely at one and the same time. Certainly, not every university fits the entrepreneurial model. There are universities that are focused primarily on teaching or research, that are not interested in commercializing discoveries or participating in schemes for social improvement. Nevertheless, there is a global movement toward the transformation of academic institutions of various kinds (e.g. teaching colleges, research universities, polytechnics etc.) into entrepreneurial universities.

The entrepreneurial university has a strong degree of autonomy to set its own strategic direction, and participate with other institutional spheres, on an equal basis, in formulating joint projects for economic and social development, especially at the regional level. The entrepreneurial university also incorporates the traditional critical functions of the university, typically exercised by students and a minority of faculty members. Critique may be focused on university functions, including university workers' rights, commercialization activities, and research goals, as well as other aspects of society. That these various functions may coexist in tension as well as cooperation is part of the strength of the academic ethos.

The entrepreneurial university model has been extended from engineering and business activities to social objectives. The Brazilian case has developed this potential most clearly through incubator projects directed at social inclusion. Realizing that the potential of the incubator for forming organizations extends well beyond high-tech, and even the business firm, the incubator process has become a means of developing the relationship of the university to heretofore excluded sectors of society. The direction of the entrepreneurial university in other countries depends upon the values the university and society wish to realize. A strong emphasis on wealth creation, as is now current in the UK, is only one direction for academic development. Universities may undertake business and social development goals simultaneously, as in Brazil.

The second academic revolution

An entrepreneurial university might seem to be an oxymoron, an antithesis of the ivory tower academic model. We usually think of an entrepreneur as an individual who takes great risks to initiate a new activity while organizations typically perform the function of institutionalizing and perpetuating an activity. Yet the university and other knowledge-producing institutions are viewed as generators of future economic growth in ever more direct ways. Academic entrepreneurship is an extension of teaching and research activities, on the one hand, and the internalization of technology transfer capabilities, taking a role traditionally played by industry, on the other.

The medieval university remit was the preservation and transmission of knowledge. The research university can be traced to the Humboldtian reform of the late 19th century, emphasizing the interconnection between teaching and research, the codification of culture and the formation of the nation state.[4] The first academic revolution was the ongoing transition from a teaching to a research institution from the mid-19th century.[5] The second academic revolution is the university's assumption of an economic and social development mission.[6]

The university is no longer the university of the Middle Ages, an isolated community of scholars. It is no longer the university of the late 19th century, whether constituted according to the land grant or to the basic research model. Translating the "land grant" model for a new era, the university is currently taking up a more fundamental role in society, one that makes it crucial to future innovation, job creation, economic growth, and sustainability. This is why the university is now being focused upon as an increasingly important social institution. It is why it can be said to be playing as important a role as C. Wright Mills argued that the military played in relation to federal government and industry during the Cold War.[7]

The transition to the entrepreneurial university enhances traditional academic missions just as new missions are enhanced by their association with old ones. The first academic mission of education inspires a second mission of research that in turn propels a third mission of economic and social development. The entrepreneurial university is a growing contemporary phenomenon, with academia taking a leading role in an emerging mode of production based on continuing organizational and technological innovation. This new mission is realized in different ways in various countries, depending upon previous academic traditions.

Universalization of academic entrepreneurship

The US entrepreneurial university is a direct outgrowth of each professor's responsibility to fund their research. Entrepreneurship thus became a defining characteristic of US academia prior to the appearance of opportunities to commercialize knowledge. Nevertheless, a wide variety of universities, including those traditionally most isolated from societal concerns, are also making the transition to an entrepreneurial mode. In Africa, the entrepreneurial model has emerged as the university has stepped in to solve national technological crises, creating spin-off firms as an unintended consequence. In Brazil, entrepreneurial education has spread throughout the university as part of an effort to encourage students in all fields to engage in innovation.

Encouraging the university to play a greater role in economic and social development is a common policy trend, with countries borrowing program and policy ideas from one another. In Europe the commercialization of research has typically emerged as a top-down assignment from national government.[8] Entrepreneurship is typically introduced in European universities by training students to carry out firm-formation activities rather than expecting the professor to take the lead. Entrepreneurial training is also a growing phenomenon in US PhD programs and European academic entrepreneurs may increasingly be found in the UK, Spain, and elsewhere, so these two modes are certainly not mutually exclusive.

A dual overlapping network of academic research groups and start-up firms, crosscut with alliances among large firms, universities, and the start-ups themselves, appears to be the emerging pattern of academic–business intersection in biotechnology, computer science, and similar fields. An enhanced university role in innovation also involves the creation of new business concepts. Some of them may derive from formal research, like biotechnology from recombinant DNA. However, like the Google search engine, they may also arise from informal interactions among colleagues that result in a new idea. It has taken a further step of creating organizational and educational innovations within the university and through collaboration with external groups, such as business angel networks, to put academic ideas with industrial potential into practice.

Making patents from academic research and licensing them to firms through a technology transfer office is one method; creating spin-off firms, in an incubator facility, is another.

More than 200 US universities currently maintain technology transfer offices to facilitate the commercialization of research. Patents and licenses based on academic discoveries contribute over 40 billion dollars to the US economy and more than 300 firms were established based directly upon academic research in 1999. These economic outcomes were based on disclosures of commercial potential in research findings that academic scientists made to their universities.[9]

Polyvalent knowledge

Faculty members, in both traditional and newly emerging science and engineering disciplines, increasingly view their research from a dual perspective of disciplinary contribution and practical use. Academic scientists who have participated in the formation of firms typically look at their research in progress through a new lens. They have learned to take the perspective of the venture capitalists that they interact with during the firm-formation process to identify commercial opportunities in their research projects. Rather than driving the university to short-term research goals, this new wave of interest in commercializing typically derives from basic research.

The potential for commercialization provides an additional impetus to long-term research projects that have potential for discontinuous innovation. A closing time gap between discovery and utilization, with the potential to enhance competitiveness and other changes in knowledge production, arises primarily from dynamics within the knowledge sphere itself. These drive these changes in the role of the university, making it a more fundamental institution for industrial productivity.

The underlying substrate for the emergence of an entrepreneurial university that retains the classic features of the "ivory tower" research university is the growth of polyvalent research fields with simultaneous theoretical, technological, and commercial potential.[10] The recognition that knowledge is imbued with multiple attributes has encouraged the multiple roles both of academics and their involvement in biotechnology firms and of industrial researchers in academic pursuits. Univalent knowledge follows a sequence from basic to applied research, typically carried out in different time periods, at different sites, and by different persons. The emergence of polyvalent knowledge has called forth the concept of translational research (a fuzzier notion than applied research) and an activity that is closely associated with fundamental investigation and is more likely to be conducted in tandem. The unitary nature of knowledge also provides a framework for reconciling multiple academic missions and making them complementary.

In previous eras, academic type—public/private, technological/liberal arts, land grant/non-land grant—explained much of the different stances of universities toward industrial involvement. Similarly, discipline type—engineering/basic research—provided between schools a clear distinction that could predict the presence or relative absence of industrial ties. A tectonic shift occurred with the emergence of biotechnology from molecular biology. Some observers view this as a relatively unique and isolated development.[11] However, it appears that the physical sciences are undergoing a similar transformation with the emergence of nanotechnology as a field with conjoint theoretical, technological, and commercial implications. Moreover, some new disciplines, such as computer science, which grew as a synthesis of engineering and basic research, had this dual characteristic from their inception and a second-order synthesis may also be identified in the emergence of proto-disciplines such as bio-informatics.

Origins of the entrepreneurial university

The formation of firms out of research activities at MIT and Harvard took place as early as the late 19th century in the fields of industrial consulting and scientific instrumentation.[12] However, these commercial entities were viewed as anomalies rather than as a normal outcome of academic research activities. Until the past two decades this skeptical view of firm-formation was taken for granted by most faculty members and administrators at liberal-arts research universities, as well. In recent years liberal-arts universities have revised their view, making firm-formation part of the academic enterprise through the formulation of policies regulating faculty participation and the establishment of administrative mechanisms such as licensing offices and incubator facilities to encourage the trend.

Although the formation of firms by academics is not a new phenomenon, it is only recently that universities have encouraged their staff to take this step. Moreover, faculty members who participate in the formation of firms are also retaining their faculty positions, after taking a leave to start the firm. MIT was the first academic institution during the early postwar era, followed by Stanford, to have a significant number of faculty members participate in the organization of firms, creating an entrepreneurial culture at these universities that encouraged other faculty members and graduate students to emulate their actions.

The entrepreneurial university emerged from two apparently contradictory 19th-century university development strategies: the land grant university, including schools to improve agriculture, such as Berkeley, and industry, such as MIT, and the classic ivory tower universities, such as Johns Hopkins and Chicago, based on pure research. The research and land grant university modes, existing in parallel until quite recently, have converged due to the increasing relevance of basic research to technological and industrial development.

As the university takes on a new role in society, it undergoes internal changes to integrate new functions and relationships. The "inner logic" of the original academic mission has been widened from knowledge conservation (education) to include also knowledge creation (research) and then application of this new knowledge (entrepreneurship). Each successive academic organizational innovation has given the university an enhanced ability to set its own strategic direction. The research university emerged as a distinctive institutional format in the mid-19th century, bringing together two activities, teaching and research, that had developed separately in colleges and scientific societies.

German state governments played a crucial role in developing the research university during the 18th century, using their control of the university appointments process to make research accomplishment the decisive criterion. Professors were appointed and laboratories were supported, even over the objections of university authorities. German state governments, initially aware of the contribution a distinguished university faculty could make to national prestige, soon also became aware of the contribution science could make to economic development and funded it for that reason.[13]

The development of university–industry connections in Germany occurred despite the increasing appeal of the pure-science ideal to many academic scientists. Many of the early German chemical manufacturers had been trained as chemists in the universities and that, no doubt, made it easier for them to relate to chemists who had remained in academia. It also made them aware of the worth of an academic connection for the scientists in their employ.

The social context of German academic science of that era is also instructive. The pharmaceutical origins of early German academic chemistry conditioned its practitioners to seek practical applications of their research skills. The apothecary connection to business provided a framework for these chemists in which to think of developing chemical products for sale, as a pharmacist of that era would develop and market a medical preparation. Nor did the terms of university appointment, at that time, appear to preclude commercial ventures. Indeed, the German state governments who were the ultimate employers of academic chemists justified their sponsorship of the discipline by the ability of its practitioners to originate useful products. The sporadic instances in which the German state governments initiated manufacturing operations upon professors' recommendations and provided financial backing for professors' ventures prefigure the more systematic current efforts of American state governments to use academic science for economic development.

The mid-19th-century German ventures were an anomaly, not an antecedent of current developments. Although close consulting relationships were established and maintained, especially between academic chemists and the chemical industry, the civil service status of the German professoriate precluded firm-formation. Thus there were no developmental links between efforts such as Liebig's and the current situation.

The development of university–industry relations

Contemporary university–industry relations emanate from two distinct sources and an emerging third hybrid stream:

1   basic research interests funded by research councils and similar bodies;
2   an industrial project for which academic input is solicited; and
3   joint formulation of research programs with conjoint basic and applied goals and multiple funding sources.

Each of these orientations to research has its organizational correlate, even if they overlap and are not mutually exclusive. Basic research takes place in research groups that function as "quasi-firms," science parks provide a home for research units of firms offering projects and collaborative opportunities to their academic counterparts, and centers provide a format to link research groups and firm researchers in a larger whole with a joint decision-making structure. A larger whole is created out of these elements as cognitive and organizational elements following the forward linear and reverse linear paths intersect and cross-fertilize each other.

As a third mission of contributing to economic and social development through technology transfer is integrated into the university in various ways, dissemination of academic knowledge takes place through patents as well as publication. The reward structure of academia has only just begun to be adjusted to accommodate this expansion in modes of dissemination. For example, Stanford recently changed its promotion criteria to credit patenting activity. The source of this change may be traced to the rise of an entrepreneurial academic to the presidency of the university. A similar event occurred at MIT with respect to consulting activity, when Vannevar Bush acceded to the deanship of the Engineering School in an earlier era.[14] He turned down a committee report placing consultation under severe restrictions, saying that these were not the terms under which he had been recruited to MIT.

There are internal and external impetuses to this transformation. On the one hand, the increasing financial resources required for the conduct of research inevitably led scientists to pay more attention to the tasks of fund-raising, and success at these tasks increasingly became a prerequisite for the ability to achieve success in research. On the other hand, opportunities for commercialization appeared in the meandering stream of research and an increasing number of scientists, from the early 20th century, have found it productive to enhance their research programs with the input of industrial as well as disciplinary questions. Moreover, from the 1930s the regions and then the federal and state governments began to view the university, supported by venture capital instruments and incubator facilities, as a source of economic development and renewal.

The first step toward an academic entrepreneurial ethos is increased sensitivity to results with practical potential, followed by a willingness to participate in the realization of this potential.[15] This change often occurs because outsiders pay attention to academic research for this very reason. The next step to an entrepreneurial academic ethos is the realization that working on practical problems posed by non-academics can have a dual potential. On the one hand, such work meets the needs of supporters of the academic enterprise and provides support to that enterprise. On the other hand, these research tasks for others may lead to the posing of new research questions with theoretical potential.

The entrepreneurial university joins a reverse linear dynamic of input from society to the classic linear model of disciplinary advance. Once the two processes operate in tandem—often through the university's technology transfer office, moving relevant knowledge and technology out of the university, bringing problems in—an interactive process is generated in which each linear starting point enhances the other. The university's incubator facility, housing both firms generated from academic research and firms brought into the university's orbit by entrepreneurs seeking enhancement through a closer connection to the academic scene, exemplifies the interactive dynamic.

A two-way flow of influence is created between the university and an increasingly knowledge-based society as the distance between institutional spheres is reduced. Universities negotiate partnerships with start-up firms emanating from academic research in which they invest intellectual and financial capital in exchange for equity. They also make broad arrangements with R & D-intensive firms for funds in exchange for preferred access to patent rights and adjunct faculty status for company researchers. The content and formats for teaching, research, and linkage itself are also affected. The assumption of an active role in economic development leaves existing academic missions in place, but it also encourages them to be carried out in new ways.

The development of technology transfer typically begins with a liaison office, going a step beyond producing trained graduates and publications to take knowledge out of the university. Universities have established liaison offices to facilitate contacts, formalizing the process by which firms often make their own contacts through former students and personal connections. An individual liaison officer may take responsibility for organizing interactions between a department or research unit and a group of interested firms. This may take the form of individual meetings, possibly leading to consultation contracts or presentations of a unit's work, typically through graduate student talks, to a group of firms on a regular basis.

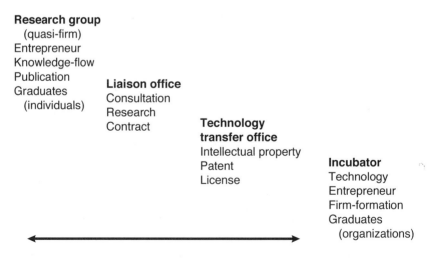

Figure 2.1 The evolution of university technology transfer capabilities.

In a second stage, the university develops the organizational capacity to patent, market, and license intellectual property. The technology transfer office operates as a dual search mechanism, pulling technology out of university research groups on the one hand, and finding a place for it on the other. In recent years universities have explored various ways to add value to early-stage university technologies by conducting marketing surveys, seeking development support, and embodying the technology in a firm.

In a third stage, knowledge and technology are embodied in a firm and moved out of the university by an entrepreneur. Firm-formation from academic research was an informal activity for many years, beginning with instrumentation companies arising from work at MIT and Harvard in the late 19th century. The initial formalization of this process took place through the invention of the venture capital firm, which provided an external support structure for firm-formation projects that were often initially located in available space in academic buildings. The incubator, a formal organization providing space and other assistance to nascent firms emanating from academic research, was introduced during the early 1980s at Renssellear Polytechnic Institute, a school (in Troy, New York) lacking a tradition of firm-formation, and has been widely utilized since.

The university as entrepreneur

To be an entrepreneur, a university has to have a considerable degree of independence from the state and industry but also a high degree of interaction with these institutional spheres. If a university system operates as it formerly did in Sweden, where the Ministry of Higher Education decided how many students would be admitted each year to each discipline, there is hardly the possibility to have sufficient autonomy on which to base an entrepreneurial university. The first requisite is that the university has some control over its own strategic direction.[16]

The second requisite is that it is in close interaction with the other spheres, that it is not an ivory tower university isolated from society. This means that the university takes a strategic view of its own development and its relationship with potential partners, but there is much more to it than that. On the one hand the relationship of the university with society changes, while on the other hand there is a renovation of the internal structure of the university. The classical teaching college still exists in the US and Ireland, but we shall treat it as a peripheral "first" cell in our model of the entrepreneurial university. However, it is the original stem cell of academia, the base from which universities have been built until quite recently, when a new line of academic development, a fourth cell, has emerged from science parks and firms, from a base rooted in economic activities rather than from a teaching and educational base rooted in the preservation and transmission of knowledge.

The transitional entrepreneurial university

The first variant of the entrepreneurial university is in a transitional phase from the research university. Thus the transitional entrepreneurial university, cell two in our table, continues to operate with problem formulation and research goals as internal processes that take place within scientific disciplines and academic research groups. What is different is that the economically and socially useful results from the so-called "meandering stream of basic research" are taken into account and specific steps are taken to see that they are utilized. A series of organizational mechanisms (e.g. liaison and patent offices) are created to arrange their transfer across the strong boundaries still existing between the university and the larger society. The innovation model is an assisted linear model, with transfer mechanisms, in contrast to the classic research university, based on a pure linear model in which knowledge flows through graduated students, publications, and conferences.

The full-fledged entrepreneurial university

The most important characteristic of the full-fledged entrepreneurial university is that research-problem definition comes from outside sources as well as from within the university and scientific disciplines. In its fullest form the definition of research problems arises as a joint project from an interaction between university researchers and external sources. Indeed, what would have been considered "external" in the previous model is less so when boundaries are reduced. Just as there is a two-way flow between teaching and research in the classic research university model, so too there is now a two-way flow between research and economic and social activities. Although quantitative data are limited, a significant but continually expanding group of academic scientists and engineers, and disciplines and subdisciplines, engage in industrial interactions that transcend traditional dissemination of knowledge.[17]

The entrepreneurial university takes the initiative to put knowledge to use. There are various organizational mechanisms for this purpose that work differently in different countries. Ownership rights to intellectual property can be shared among inventors and the university, as they are in the US; in Sweden they are entirely owned by the professor. However, university "holding companies" have been established to buy those rights and commercialize them. As the university becomes involved in technology transfer and firm-formation, it attains a new entrepreneurial identity. This is part of a long-term trend in which business expertise, formerly localized within the university in extra-academic functions, is extended to traditional academic fields.

The third cell is a new entrepreneurial university, organized on the base of a science park, research institute, or group of firms. Such academic institutions have begun as an extension of a firm or research institute. Examples include the PhD program in the policy sciences sponsored by the RAND Corporation in the US and the development of the Blekinge Institute of Technology on the base of the Soft Center science park in Karlskronna Ronneby, Sweden. In this model knowledge-based economic activity precedes the development of academic work, which is then built upon and closely tied to its originating source. The university, at least in its initial phases, is an extension of the science park, research institute, or group of firms. Eventually the academic activities may grow into a fully fledged entrepreneurial university.

The fourth cell is the integration of entrepreneurial activities into the regular academic work of the university. This means that entrepreneurial training is available to all students. Just as students learn to write a personal essay to express their thoughts, a scientific paper to test hypotheses against evidence, so they should learn to write a business plan to set forth a project to accomplish, a method to reach that goal, and a market test. Furthermore, just as the laboratory is alongside the classroom, so should the incubator facility be part of each academic department, with the incubator—as a trainer of organizations—seen as an educational as well as an economic-development arm of the university. The full-fledged entrepreneurial university is a seamless web of teaching, research, and entrepreneurial activities, with each supporting the other.

The legitimization of academic entrepreneurship

Organizational mechanisms for technology transfer, invented earlier in the 20th century at MIT, have since spread to a broader range of academic institutions. The American model was institutionalized in 1980 by amendment to the Patent and Trademark Law, the Bayh-Dole Act, through which the US Congress turned over to universities intangible intellectual property arising from federally supported academic research.

The Bayh-Dole Act of 1980 resolved the contradiction between government ownership of intellectual-property rights in the research that it funded at universities and the wish to see those rights put to use. Bayh-Dole created an intellectual-property development system that combined private and public benefits in a balanced framework. The Bayh-Dole regime took into account the need to incentivize all participants to simultaneously advance commercialization and maximize access to knowledge created with government funds. While university technology transfer pre-dates Bayh-Dole and was on an upward trajectory at the time of its passage, the act codified and legitimized a set of informal practices and relationships that had emerged among university, industry, and government during the preceding century.

The act resolved the free-rider problems that companies faced in dealing with government-owned, university-originated intellectual property. A firm feared that if it went ahead and spent considerable sums developing a successful technology then a second firm would come along and demand access on the grounds that the technology had been funded with taxpayer monies. By placing this intellectual property securely within the university, a firm could be guaranteed that when an exclusive license was granted, it would hold. Technology transfer offices uniformly accept the validity and necessity of the law. Not only does it provide a basis for technology transfer, it also encourages faculty to participate since they are guaranteed a significant share of the income, in contrast to corporate employees who are at the mercy of their employer.

Academic transformation and continuity

A major reason for this broadening of the university's role was its cost-effectiveness: combining research and teaching was far less expensive than maintaining separate institutions for each purpose, as became commonplace in Europe. Nevertheless, although some still lament the emphasis that universities now place on research, proponents of expanding the university's mission have for the most part been vindicated on pedagogical grounds. The knowledge generated by faculty members' research infuses their teaching with relevance and vitality. Opposition to universities' new entrepreneurial role is likely to undergo a similar evolution. For, as in the case of disputes over faculty involvement in research, conflicts of interest over the commercialization of research are symptoms of change in academic mission.

Maintaining boundaries between public science and private appropriation is becoming less of an issue than developing technology transfer formats that enhance research as well as commercialization. Technology transfer offices find that they have to expand their role by assisting faculty members in obtaining research funds to explore the technological implications of their research in order to arrive at a patent application. Once protection of intellectual property is achieved, such offices often find that in order to move a technology into use they have to extend themselves beyond marketing licenses to assist in firm-formation, even if the long-term objective is transfer to an existing firm.

Once academic research is defined as a marketable good and treated as intellectual property, the traditional forms of dissemination, such as publication in academic journals and presentations at conferences, persist. Indeed, having a paper published in a major journal can help a company seeking funds and even increase the value of its stock. As universities become entrepreneurs, they do not give up their previous functions of teaching and disinterested research. Academic research groups and science-based start-ups exist along a continuum, with attention to rewards of recognition and finance. University spin-offs find it to their advantage in attracting investors to participate in the elaboration of the original discovery, and publish together with their academic collaborators. Licensing, joint ventures, marketing, and sales of products provide additional venues for knowledge dissemination to broader areas of society, above and beyond publication.

The norms of the entrepreneurial university

The entrepreneurial academic model can be expressed in five norms. These norms for entrepreneurship and their opposites are in fruitful tension with each other. The optimal result will be reached when there is a balance between them. They may serve as guidelines for the transformation of academic institutions.

1   *Capitalization*. Knowledge is created and transmitted for use as well as for disciplinary advance; the capitalization of knowledge becomes the basis for economic and social development and thus of an enhanced role for the university in society.
2   *Interdependence*. The entrepreneurial university interacts closely with industry and government; it is not an ivory tower isolated from society.
3   *Independence*. The entrepreneurial university is a relatively independent institution; it is not a dependent creature of another institutional sphere.
4   *Hybridization*. The resolution of the tensions between the principles of interdependence and independence is an impetus to the creation of hybrid organizational formats to realize both objectives simultaneously.
5   *Reflexivity*. There is a continuing renovation both of the internal structure of the university as its relation to industry and government changes and of that of industry and government as their relationships with the university are revised.

Conclusion

The transformation of academia from a "secondary" to a "primary" institution is an unexpected outcome of the institutional development of modern society.[18] In consequence, "the knowledge industry in modern societies is no longer a minor affair run by an intellectual elite, an activity that might be considered by pragmatic leaders as expendable; it is a mammoth enterprise on a par with heavy industry, and just as necessary to the country in which it is situated."[19] The location of academic research was previously of little account since results, embodied in papers and publications, could be seen to be capable of flowing anywhere. As the practical implications of research arise ever closer in time to the making of a discovery, the location of research becomes a political issue, relevant to every local economy. It leads government, at different levels, as well as companies and universities themselves, to explore ways for knowledge-producing institutions to make a greater contribution to the economy and to society.

Increased knowledge production does not translate readily into increased economic productivity, even given a decent respect for the time requirements of knowledge flows across institutional, political, and organizational boundaries. A more hands-on approach to innovation is being introduced in countries and regions at different levels of scientific, economic, and social development. Innovation analysts have examined the sources and consequences of these efforts, without reaching consensus on the relationship between research and outcomes. There is only a presumption that the relationship is strengthening, or can be strengthened, even when it is weak. The Swedish paradox of high R & D spending with an apparently relatively low return from this investment exemplifies a broader innovation paradox—gaps in the relationships between science, technology, and industry—that manifests itself in different situations.

In the US there is a gap between research and development, the so-called "valley of death" that is only partially filled by public venture capital. In Brazil, despite a growing incubator movement, there is an insufficient supply of high-tech start-ups to utilize the public funds that have recently become available to jump-start a venture capital industry. On the other hand, the UK has until quite recently starved its universities of research funding, calling into question the viability of its science base as a platform for innovation. Developing countries have to contend with a broader range of gaps, given a weaker institutional infrastructure. Nevertheless, for various historical reasons universities have been established in virtually every part of the world, making available a potential platform for knowledge-based innovation.

3 The evolution of the firm

Firm-formation is increasingly central to innovation strategy. The typical large-firm innovation decision-making process compares present profits from existing technologies with the difficult start-up phase of products based on new technology. The investment required by the new product is balanced against profits that might be made from further investment in existing products and the latter path is usually taken. The potential for the new product cannibalizing the market for the old is another counterweight to internal innovation. Some firms, like GE, that formerly based their growth on new products emanating from research have, in recent decades, given up this strategy in favor of acquisition.[1]

Sometimes top management, does not comprehend the potential of its lab's accomplishments. Xerox believed its PARC Lab advances in computer technology were too far removed from the firm's business in document reproduction. Failure to pursue innovation may inspire employees to leave and start a firm based on the new technology. Indeed, a large firm may recognize the efficacy of spin-off, assist the process, and take a share of the equity in return. Even when a firm opposes the process and brings a lawsuit against its former employees, an agreement is typically negotiated that recognizes the validity of the spin-off with a payment to the originating firm. For example, Texas Instrument tried and failed to halt the exodus of members of its personal computer development group who founded the Compaq corporation in the early 1980s.

As industrial firms downsize, the knowledge-based firm, as a spin-out from either an existing firm or an academic research group, is emerging as an engine of economic growth. Growing a new firm from indigenous advanced research, rather than attracting a branch plant from elsewhere, is increasingly recognized as a superior strategy. Failure is nobody's child but new firms often spring out of a failed start-up in a fission process. Knowledge-based firms also often have a prehistory in which their format is akin to an academic research project. This chapter discusses the enhancement of the knowledge-based firm-formation process through interaction with university and government.

The firm in the triple helix

Entrepreneurial universities, far-sighted governments, and existing firms increasingly pursue growth strategies based on academic innovation and incubation.[2] As firms seek discontinuous innovation they tend to partner, first with entities similar to themselves and then with more dissimilar organizations, like large pharmaceutical firms with biotech start-ups and university centers. More recently, large firms have moved units to science parks in order to collaborate more closely with academic research groups to develop new products as well as to recruit and keep an eye on discoveries with commercial implications.[3]

High-tech firm-formation is typically the result of an entrepreneurial process that has inputs from multiple sources. Nevertheless, it is often an individual with a new vision for recombining existing elements in a new way, or the inventor or innovator of a far-reaching technology who possesses highly developed social skills, like Thomas A. Edison or Bill Gates, who becomes the exponent of a new industrial or service sector. However, other contributions to firm-formation are often forgotten, given the tendency in the US to focus on the individual entrepreneur rather the entrepreneurial process that typically involves a group of people with complementary technical and business skills.[4]

Behind the simple story of the capturing of an opportunity by a single heroic entrepreneur, there is almost always a more complex tale of the development of highly skilled human capital, resistance from established structures, and support from a variety of government programs, and a decade, or more, of firm-formation struggle. The story of firm-formation as a collaborative process is told more readily in communal societies such as Sweden where an entrepreneurial initiative is explicitly a collective decision. Indeed, the project typically does not go forward without a group behind it. But is that process really so different from the one that led Paul Allen and Bill Gates to leave Harvard after their first year in order to catch the wave of the personal-computer revolution?

Firms appearing out of academia usually keep close contact with their source of origin, resulting in an industrial penumbra surrounding the university. In nascent US high-tech regions, there may also be colocation on campus of firm and academic research groups, with representatives of government programs visiting regularly or operating from local offices nearby.[5] A new mode of production, based on academic research and triple helix relations, is emerging out of the chrysalis of innovation systems focused on the firm.

The emergence of the triple helix firm

The American model of knowledge commercialization is based on connecting the patent system to the intellectual output of the university research group, on the one hand, and integrating the research group into an organizational network of transfer offices, incubator facilities, and venture capital firms, on the other. Initially, at MIT this process used the traditional academic committee to review inventions and an intermediary organization, the research corporation, to market the patents to industry. The next step was the creation of an organization within the university, the technology transfer office, to carry out this task on a more intensive basis.

In either format, either as a branch of the university or as a free-standing entity, a search mechanism was introduced to identify commercializable knowledge within the university and to market it to potential users. Although these mechanisms were often created to move knowledge and technology to existing firms, there has been a gradual shift in focus to the start-up process, both to maximize revenues and to find an outlet for knowledge and technology that is beyond the purview of existing firms. During the 1930s Stanford University operated a "patent pool" on behalf of electronics firms that had either spun out from the university or were working closely with it. This practice exemplifies a collaborative innovation strategy linking a university and a group of firms whose product development efforts were largely based on university inventions.

The essence of the US multilayered system, drawing on inputs and support from academia and government at various levels, is a focus on firm-formation in emerging technology areas. Reducing risk and compressing time frames in the transition of knowledge to utilization is the primary objective. The period of gestation for high-tech growth firms based on discontinuous innovation is relatively long, typically at least a decade. Firms with genuine innovations in business models and technology take a slower route than "copycats" that do not rely on innovation. It is a path that, due to its extended time frame, often eschews private in favor of public venture capital, by necessity or design.

The "bright" side of the venture capital model is driven by the potential for industrial and social innovation that new technologies, such as the electric light in the late 19th century and nanotechnology at present, make possible. The "dark" side came to the forefront during the late 1990s when venture capitalists eschewed a relatively long-term strategy of five or more years to exit in 18 or even 12 months. A technology entrepreneur noted in a personal interview

> If you look at successful companies, there has been a big shakeout. Enormous amounts of investment were done. Look at the companies left standing. Most of those companies did not get early investments. They were able to slowly develop their technical and business teams, gain experience in their markets, make their mistakes; get over them.

Often, government R & D funds provided the means to get through the so-called valley of death, between proof of the concept of a technology and achievement of a stable revenue stream from product sales. A technology entrepreneur in a field that was "out of favor" with venture capital during the bubble said in a personal interview, "It was clear that nobody was investing in the company so I decided to get a government grant."

Firm-formation, based on new technology, involves a process of technical and business partners getting acquainted, building trust, and forming long-term alliances. Cross-fertilization between the two perspectives is also the key to innovation. The building of creative relationships between technical and business people is an essential part of a firm-formation process that is much more than a simple investment of funds in exchange for a share of ownership in a start-up firm. A business partner may realize a technology has implications that were not seen by the technical entrepreneur or, even if noted by them, may not have been viewed as feasible to follow up until the suggestion came from the partner.

The establishment of a balanced technology–business collaboration during the firm-formation process is the key to the creation of a start-up with significant growth potential, rather than a firm focused on research or technology development. A technology entrepreneur said in a personal interview that for her firm,

> The key event was when a small investment bank decided to help me create a company. I had a software technology for children and was marching around to potential investors. I always knew that business applications was a possibility but did not think I was credible at creating that business. So when they said that was what they wanted to do, that is when we started the company.

The involvement of a university faculty as a collaborator, as well as the investment bank, enhanced the nascent firm's credibility on both the research and market sides, helping it to obtain an advanced-technology development grant.

Government, university, and the private sector play various roles, in different combinations, to assist firm-formation and growth in the US. Nevertheless, despite the decades-long existence of government support for firm-formation, the concept of public venture capital is relatively unknown, and is even viewed as a contradiction in terms. Although this perception is changing, many technology entrepreneurs still cannot imagine that government programs can provide funds that can help them start a firm and so do not apply. Several years ago, two workshops were held simultaneously at a software industry conference; the one on private venture capital attracted a large number of people and the other, on public venture capital, attracted only a very few including two innovation researchers.[6]

Since relatively few Americans are willing to admit the considerable role that government plays in knowledge commercialization, given the strong cultural emphasis on the individual entrepreneur and the private sector, the idea of university and government as a source of economic initiative tends to be suppressed. A strong ideological tradition presumes that the successful entrepreneur arises from humble circumstances, like a character in a "Horatio Alger" story. Even William Gates of Microsoft, scion of a prominent Seattle family, is subsumed into this myth. Just as an American system of manufactures, based on interchangeable parts in machines, was identified in the mid-19th century, a triple helix of university, industry, and government, each "taking the role of the other" in society, can be identified today.

The firm in the university

The phenomenon of firm-formation from academic research has its roots in the way that research was institutionalized in American universities from the mid-19th century. Professors, already paid for teaching duties, assumed research responsibilities. With modest financial support, graduate students assisted professors at the same time as they received their training. Students entered the laboratories and left with their degrees within relatively few years, creating a continual stream of new people with new ideas going in both directions from university to industry and vice versa. Based upon the premise that industrial interaction was essential for a great school, encouraging firm-formation was part of a strategy for developing the Stanford Engineering School which was located at a rural site in the late 19th century.

This system was productive and cost-effective due to the low rates of pay and the high level of results obtained. It expanded in a modest way, with support from foundation and industry in the early 20th century. In the post-World War II era, a huge decentralized research infrastructure has arisen, spanning old and newly emerging research universities. Scaled up to support military research at a few leading universities during World War II, expansion of the academic research system is currently driven by the desire to renew the economic base of every part of the country. Research universities consist of a series of such "quasi-firms," often aggregated into centers, linking groups to achieve larger theoretical and practical objectives simultaneously.

As recently as the early postwar period, the concentration of research at a few leading universities on the East and West Coasts, and a few Midwestern schools, could be accepted on the grounds that knowledge could flow freely to wherever it was needed. However, once it was widely recognized, as early as the 1960s, that new industrial agglomerations in electronics and computers, and then in biotechnology, were appearing adjacent to universities that had attained early distinction in these fields, the race was on to found or enhance local universities elsewhere explicitly to attain that goal.

Academic scientists, perforce, had to focus on the organizational and economic aspects of research, even apart from involvement in commercialization. Professors are typically compelled to remove themselves from the bench to devote virtually all their time to organizational and intellectual tasks as the size of the group increases to seven or eight members. At this scale, the professor has become a research manager, even though he or she is still an academic and is officially called an "individual investigator." Often persons in this situation describe themselves as "running a small business," since they see themselves as responsible not only for their own funding but for that of several other people.

These developments laid the groundwork for the contemporary phenomenon of the formation of firms by scientists who treat scientific discoveries as marketable goods. It is not a long step from running a quasi-firm to starting an actual firm. Indeed, scientists involved in the organization of research groups, firms, and centers sometimes say that they do more "business" in managing a center than in running a start-up.

European professors, by contrast, have had less impetus to be entrepreneurial until quite recently. Research funds were attached to the position. Junior faculty members were expected to work for senior faculty. This is in sharp contrast to the US assistant professor, who has the responsibility to seek research support from the time of their initial appointment. Given these strong differences in academic traditions, European universities wishing to foster entrepreneurship have established training programs designed to create firms as well as educate students in the new discipline.

The focus on educating entrepreneurs and training groups of students as firms may explain some of the recent rise in high-tech firm-formation in Sweden, a country previously noted for its concentration of large mid-level technology firms. A tightly knit group of firms and families has provided a core economic structure in Sweden for decades. Following the introduction of mechanical industry in the 19th century, a relatively small number of firms have dominated each industrial sector.[7] Historically an implicit public–private agreement to keep wages relatively low, allowing firms to retain a relatively high portion of profits, in exchange for social welfare benefits from government provided a stable economic and social foundation until quite recently. However, a hemorrhage that could not be staunched developed from the 1970s, with the decline of traditional industries like shipbuilding and textiles and the emigration of some firms or loss of control of others to foreign owners.

The apparent need to create a new generation of entrepreneurial firms as a source of growth has become increasingly central to the economic and political agenda. The establishment of entrepreneurial training programs in universities and the emergence of popular music and software sectors augurs the beginnings of a new economy, based on various intangible goods, organized as economic entities in non-traditional formats.

The university in the firm

A special graduation ceremony of firms from the incubator facility at the Pontifical Catholic University of Rio de Janeiro exemplifies the crossover of the university's economic development mission with its teaching mission. The event marked the departure of firms from the university's incubator, "Project Genesis." The incubator follows the academic training model by mandating the firm to stay for a limited period of 2–3 years before "graduation" and movement to a commercial location.

The rector opened the ceremony with a brief mass and speech about realizing dreams. A representative of each firm came forward to tell what had been accomplished during the time in the incubator. Most firms focused on software development emanating from computer science; some maintained links to academic research. One company arose from an applied-physics research group—which had itself spun out of the physics department—to develop oil exploration technology. The role of the university extends after graduation through a "club" linking groups of alumni firms with potential partners, typically drawn from companies of older alumni.

While ideas for new firms continue to come from people working in large or small companies, a university research project is increasingly a source of new firm ideas in an increasing number of fields, ranging from biotechnology to finance. The role of the university in firm-formation, once considered a happenstance anomaly, is becoming a regular part of the academic enterprise. Indeed, in sponsoring entrepreneurial training programs that take groups of students through the start-up process, the university is a teacher of organizations.

The reconceptualization of firm-formation as an educational activity has been difficult to discern since it typically takes place in incubators that are usually viewed as part of the university's technology transfer activities rather than its educational mission. Nevertheless, just as the university trains individual students in classrooms and laboratories and sends them out into the world, it performs the same function for organizations in its incubator facilities.

The evolution of the firm

The production and sale of knowledge of various kinds has become a core business activity of companies such as Entelos, a small modeling firm that reverse-engineers the biological pathways of ailments for pharmaceutical firms.[8] Even as knowledge is increasingly codified as intellectual property by individual firms, the value of some kinds of knowledge depends upon it being shared across firms' boundaries, such as standards according to which a family of products (e.g. GSM mobile wireless) operates. The paradox is that an individual company standard can be worth less than one that cuts across an industry, even though no single firm controls the latter.

The dream is to virtually control a standard like Microsoft's operating system and thereby capture enormous revenues. Nevertheless, although single firms sometimes control most or all of a standard, there is typically a process of negotiation among firms, sometimes regulated by government, national or multinational, to establish a single platform on which an entire industry is built. Thus agreement on a single standard for mobile wireless in Europe gave European firms a competitive advantage over US firms, where various firms were unsuccessfully trying to impose their standard on the industry.

From the late 19th century, industrial firms shifted control over knowledge up the corporate hierarchy, removing it from worker control and placing it in a professional engineering corps under strict managerial control. While management gained increased control over the production process, the firm lost the means to utilize improvements made by production-line workers. By contrast, encouraging and rewarding worker input became a hallmark of Japanese industrial firms during the postwar era.

This process was formalized by the Japanese adoption of statistical practices originated in the US, allowing innovations made by all employees to be tracked as problems were identified and solved. The transition of industrial firms to a knowledge format parallels the evolution of the firm from an organizational format for the production of physical goods, with knowledge as an ancillary component, to the production of intangible goods, such as software, that may not have a physical embodiment.

Academic origins and government programs, at various levels, fostering university–industry collaborations to stimulate start-ups, necessitate revision in the concept of the firm. A firm is usually thought of as a business, with products going out and revenues coming in, until bankruptcy do us part. A triple helix firm based on organizational and technological innovation, occurring through networks across institutional spheres, differs from the "contractual firm," based upon transactions across discrete boundaries.[9]

Whereas the traditional firm, with strong boundaries, is a nexus of contracts negotiated to set the price for its inputs and outputs, the triple helix firm is part of a collaborative process that may include other firms and non-firm entities, such as university research groups and government agencies. The traditional vertical value chain from suppliers to customers is reconfigured as formerly vertically linked elements in such fields as software, with customers and suppliers as co-producers of services, and formerly horizontally linked elements such as knowledge, technology, and funding inputs, drawn from academia and government, now take place simultaneously and in parallel.

Embedded in relationships with these institutional spheres, the knowledge-based firm, is a departure in industrial organization. From the late 19th century, corporations focused on development, production, and marketing of tangible goods, internalizing functions, vertically as well as horizontally, making the firm less dependent upon the external world for all but the final transaction with its customers. Henry Ford carried the vertical integration of the firm to its logical conclusion with his River Rouge Plant that took in iron ore and other raw materials at one end and sent out cars, as finished products, at the other.

Ford's rival, General Motors (GM), pioneered the horizontal extension of the firm, applying a traditional military format to business. Alfred P. Sloan introduced the line and staff organization, integrating several previously independent automobile firms as divisions, with an overlay of a management and decision-support structures. GM grew and addressed different market segments without becoming unwieldy. This format also made it possible to share the cost of specialized functions, such as strategic planning and finance, between several sub-units.

In the mid-20th century the conglomerate extended the divisional structure of the large corporation from a single sector to disparate businesses, while retaining a common financial structure. For a brief period, from the 1960s to the 1980s, the multinational firm was considered to be the ultimate form of business organization. Operating across national borders, it differed from older trading companies that operated in a highly centralized fashion from the home country in that it utilized the organizational innovations of divisional and conglomerate firms. National sub-units were allowed considerable autonomy even as the multinational used differential costs of production and varying regulatory environments in each country to the firm's advantage.

As technologies were superseded in advanced industrial societies, they could be transferred to protected industrial environments in developing countries. Each of these organizational innovations appeared to lead in a unilinear direction toward increase in the scale and scope of the business firm.[10] However, even as the multi-national firm became ascendant as a bureaucratic format for integrating a multiplicity of units, an alternative scale–scope format for integrating aspects of production and distribution appeared: the cluster of small interrelated firms, specializing in different aspects of production, typically based on kinship and proximity ties, rooted in a local region.[11]

Early clusters were identified in low-tech businesses such as textiles, clothing, and leather goods, but the concept was soon applied to an agglomeration of high-tech firms that had emerged from a related set of university laboratories and research centers at such schools as MIT and Stanford. While these "technology-based firm's strength and competitive edge derive from the engineering know-how of people who are integral to the firm, and upon the subsequent transformation of this know-how into products or services for a market,"[12] such firms are often part of overarching virtual networks that transcend companies and infuse the individual firm with new sources of innovation.[13]

There has been a transition in recent years from firms linked to each other solely through competitive market relationships to strategic alliances between firms and establishment of other collaborative relations with academia and government.[14] Such knowledge-based firms typically transcend a simple business proposition. Biotechnology firms often originate as extensions of university research groups, incorporate academic practices such as postdoctoral fellowships, and contribute to the expansion of academic research, directly through research contracts and indirectly through university participation in ownership.

The transformation of the social relationship of a partnership between individuals to carry out a joint activity, producing a good or service for sale, into an abstract legal entity, the firm, allowed the life of the business to continue and expand, without the founder's participation. At a later stage, partnership re-emerges as an organizational framework among firms as they cooperate with each other and with universities, government laboratories, and other knowledge-generating institutions in order to produce knowledge-based products requiring inputs from various sources.

Schumpeter noted the transition from an informal to a formal knowledge-based company regime as a stage in firm-development. "The first thing a modern concern does as soon as it feels it can afford it is to establish a research department every member of which knows that his bread and butter depends on his success in devising improvements."[15] In addition to devising research-based improvements internally, firms have sought to access them from external sources such as independent inventors, consulting engineers, and contract research organizations established to meet industry needs, as well as universities.

Government in the firm

Two strikingly different types of high-tech firms can be identified: market-oriented firms and research-oriented firms. A government program to support innovation encouraged market-oriented firms focused on product sales to take up research to enhance their products and research oriented firms to develop collaborations to seek a market for their research results. There was a movement in both directions toward a middle ground, with research-oriented firms attempting to position themselves to produce products, and market-oriented firms pursuing more advanced research as an unintended consequence of their participation in this program.

The more advanced the technical idea on which the firm is based, the likelier it is that government money, typically coming from research programs in the US, will be the initial source of funds. Seeking job creation and research advance, government is often willing to fund start-ups with a grant or "soft loan" long before angels and venture capitalists feel ready to consider an investment. Such a firm, like a butterfly emerging from its chrysalis, is a concatenation of academic, government, and business elements. Only later, if and when innovation subsides, does it take shape as a traditional firm. As this process takes place, the role of government in triple helix firm-formation is suppressed. The US paradox is that despite having arrived at an optimum role for government in innovation, belief in the efficacy of government is low.

A government technology development award allows a firm at either end of the market–research spectrum to broaden its focus and operate in the middle ground, thus bridging the gap between product development and R & D from whichever side it has opened up. For example, a research-oriented firm may seek an alliance with a market-oriented firm to commercialize its technology. Conversely, a market-oriented firm may establish a research unit. Such an award can broaden the focus of a firm to include advanced capabilities in its products when it would otherwise not have had the resources needed.

This phenomenon was observed in a close-to-the market company, originally oriented toward developing software for individual doctors' offices and small medical practices. The firm's founders realized that the extended capabilities of its product line, made possible by a government-supported R & D project, would make its products attractive to larger vendors. Indeed, the large medical units where the firm was testing its government-enhanced product were now seen as potential customers. Thus by extending the capabilities of the product, through taking on a research orientation, the firm found that a new market opportunity opened up.

The process of expanding product development capabilities moves in the other direction for a research-oriented firm, starting from preparation of the application. Many of the market questions that need to be addressed in the proposal can be answered according to the business criteria specified in the proposal application kit. A process may thus be begun in which commercial opportunities are seriously explored.

Even if the program is initially viewed as "simply another route to a government contract," such a grant can become the first step toward a research-oriented firm eventually taking a product to market. In one case the grant did not help the research-oriented firm move as far as it had hoped toward commercialization. This was in part due to difficulties in cooperation between partners who had differing perceptions of medical software technical requirements. Nevertheless, a process of transformation was initiated. Even though government funding ended before the technology development was completed, the firm hired its own programmers, including one from the former software collaborator, in order to complete the project. To support this work, the firm entered into negotiations to raise private funding to bring the health care software to fruition.

Research-oriented firms

Companies are commonly thought of as being market-oriented. However, some firms have little connection to broader markets beyond a single customer, for example a particular agency of the government or of an individual large firm. Indeed, there is a tradition of companies that produce research results and technology to order, as government contractors. Such firms operate as research shops, producing reports, papers, patents, and "tools" that others can use in product development. Although legally companies, they have very little notion of how to go about selling a product. To qualify as a finalist for government funding, from programs with emphasis upon both business as well as technical merit, they may need to recruit a business manager, obtain advice from business consultants, or ally with other companies who have business capabilities.

Without strengthening their business capability, research-oriented firms' main hope for eventual utilization will continue to be their habitual route, that is, dissemination through papers and patents. Government programs to support advanced technology seek to add a direct commercialization component to the knowledge dissemination path. Not surprisingly, some of these companies, at first, tend to view such programs as merely another government agency contracting for technology development and assume that the firm's "research result" will satisfy the agency's requirements. However, the program's objective is a research result that can become a marketable product.

Market-oriented firms

At the other end of the spectrum are market-oriented firms that may view a government technology development award as a centerpiece of their strategy to move their technologies into the marketplace. Market-oriented companies are typically populated with collaborating practitioners with similar technical expertise, such as doctors with software coding skills, and marketing and sales experts. These firms typically have an extremely short time horizon for product development and do not usually engage in advanced research. Although such firms are "high-tech," in that they utilize state-of-the-art technology to develop high-tech products, they usually do not do early-stage research in the traditional sense of investigation that is not directly tied to immediate product development.

Market-oriented firms are typically restricted from mounting a research program by stringent finances, strategic orientation, and/or lack of appropriate personnel. These firms tend to operate with an incremental perspective toward product development, utilizing new combinations of existing technologies to solve a problem or provide a service. They consider doing research only when they can envisage that it will allow them to make a significant competitive leap forward in sales by adding a new capability or functionality to their product line. Given the concentration of available resources on short-term product development and the pressures of cash-flow balancing, they seek an external source of funding so that their existing efforts in product development will not be financially drained. Before taking on a research project, the firm's management will also want to insure that attention will not be diverted from the firm's primary goal of current product development.

"Dual-life" individuals

Knowledge-based firms are often helped to succeed by "dual-life" individuals who, whether starting from either the technical or the business side, have gained sufficient knowledge of the other side to conduct business or interpret technology. Sometimes individuals have had serious professional training on both sides, for example a molecular biologist who obtains an MBA or a lawyer who also has a technical degree. Other times, the knowledge of the other side is picked up informally, say by an MBA who has done due diligence numerous times in a technical area or by a technical person who has repeatedly become involved in business negotiations as an inventor. Of course, it is also possible for people to fool themselves, and others, into thinking they have greater expertise than they actually possess.

Dual-life persons reduce difficulties in translation from one discipline to another. Thus the presence of medical persons with significant computer knowledge has facilitated projects; absence of a computer expert with medical knowledge has slowed them down. Persons who combine two fields in new ways are a key to innovation in fields such as healthcare informatics that are in the early stages of development. By maintaining a "dual life" these individuals are able to translate between both spheres of interest, in this case computer science and medicine. By retaining their interest in the old role even as they move into a new one, a crossdisciplinary bridge for their colleagues is created.

Crossover was observed in both directions: from computer science to medicine and from medicine to computer science. A business founder, in a personal interview, described his partner, a medical doctor with a computer background, thus

> His vision is great because he sees what happens in everyday practice and can take that to help us develop products. He can say, "You know, it would really help physicians if this could happen." And that's a major contribution because the other companies don't have their finger into that.

There are more medical persons with significant computer knowledge than computer scientists with medical knowledge, although a computer scientist with a personal interest in medical issues was often an important impetus to involvement in a project.

A speech-recognition software development project, lacking such dual-life persons, exemplified the issues that could arise from lack of shared understandings. In this case the problem was different expectations of task requirements in medicine and computer science. For example, transcription of the spoken word was required to a much higher degree of precision by linguistic experts than by medical practitioners. The linguistic specialists always wanted more information, which required more work and drove up costs. The dispute was summed up by a software developer for the Dragon speech recognition firm who, in a personal interview, said, "the upside is when you get a lot more people together, you get a lot more skills. The downside is there is no central control. You know, we get in a feud about the speech data and we just sort of cut them off." In this instance, the disagreement was peremptorily resolved by a third party who was lower down in the status hierarchy of the project, namely the software programmer who had to write code based on the speech data.

The presence of translators and brokers in the collaboration process might lessen the misunderstandings that arise in unsupervised courtship between partners from different cultures of research and commerce. Indeed, some of the larger collaborative projects were supervised by a coordinating group that performed such "translation" services, among other tasks. In addition to mediation among partners from different business and technical cultures, there is also a movement toward individuals performing multiple technical and business roles. The increasing importance of knowledge to the generation of new industrial capital leads to a closer relationship between the generators of knowledge and a new generation of capitalists, some of whom are one and the same persons.

Conditions for knowledge-based firm-formation and growth

The following conditions are typically found in regions where high-technology ventures are emerging. The premise of the following model is the existence of commercial opportunities known to scientists, engineers, and other professionals. The first two sets of factors are essential to the development of knowledge-based firms; the final group of factors improves the chances that a knowledge-based economic development strategy will be realized. Universities are especially important to the creation of knowledge-based firms since they have people with many of the resources such as skills, time, and equipment to realize the initial stages of this strategy.

Human capital factors

1   A critical mass of scientists and engineers linked through social networks. Networks often link scientists among university, corporate, and government laboratories in a region.

2   The existence of research groups in areas of potential commercialization.
3   A pool of scientists and engineers interested in forming their own firms; these may be faculty members, graduate students, or scientists and engineers from government or corporate laboratories.

Material factors

4   Availability of seed capital from private or governmental sources.
5   Inexpensive and appropriate space for new firms either in underutilized industrial offices or in university buildings.
6   Equipment, ranging from multimedia computers to prototype biotechnology plants.

Organizational factors

7   Opportunities for scientists and engineers to learn business skills or gain access to persons with these skills. A graduate school of business with consulting services or courses on entrepreneurship in which students develop business plans can be helpful.
8   University policies designed to (a) encourage faculty members and students to interact with industry, (b) give academic credit for promotion and award degrees for this work, and (c) provide clear guidelines delineating appropriate activities.
9   Applied research institutes, centers, and incubator facilities to assist firms with development problems and to provide mediating linkages between academic scientists and engineers and industry.
10 A residential community with cultural, scenic, and/or recreational resources that can attract and hold a population whose skills make them potentially highly mobile.

Conclusion: the triple helix in the firm

Firm-formation allows innovation to become the central focus of the organization in a way that is rarely possible in older firms where it must compete for attention with existing technologies and businesses. An alternative organizational format based on networks of firms arising from the bottom up has appeared that is increasingly based on technological innovation in such areas as software and biotechnology. Innovation has broadened from a focus on product innovation within firms to organizational changes within the triple helix.

Cooperation among government, industrial, and academic actors can extend such innovations into a new mode of production within a region, across a national innovation system, and even more broadly. While upgrading the capabilities of small- and medium-sized firms (SMEs) and renewing large firms is still important, the dynamic of the start-up process has become more important to advancing technology, creating employment and growth.

The firm is thus transformed from a competitive unit related to other firms solely through the market to a triple helix entity increasingly based on relationships with other firms as well as academia and government. Often encouraged by government, large firms in Japan and Sweden have willingly entered new technological areas, with Saab, for example, developing medical devices in Linköping. However, the Saab case proved to be an instance of a firm's resistance to moving into an area different from its existing technologies and businesses. Indeed, Saab eventually withdrew from medical devices, unwilling to commit the resources to develop it as a new business area.

Nevertheless, the government-supported Saab initiative seeded a firm-formation dynamic in the Linköping region.[16] A municipally supported incubator provided a home for the Saab orphans. The firms were then linked to a new university, based on interdisciplinary themes, that was more receptive to industry–university links than an older, more traditional, academic foundation might have been. A culture of firm-formation and entrepreneurship thus took root in the region.

Italy also has an entrepreneurial culture but it typically does not affect the universities, due to differences in academic culture and organization. Nevertheless, there is a movement in Italy—beginning with the establishment of industrial liaison offices, incubator facilities, and collaboration of pharmaceutical firms with university laboratories—to re-create academic–industry ties, such as those that in a previous era were commonplace at Polytechnico Milan. Italy's industrial districts of low-tech firms are increasingly outmoded—they need closer ties to knowledge-producing organizations to innovate—and its mid-tech firms are in decline. Under these conditions, the university's potential as an engine of renewal for existing firms, and a source of new knowledge-based firms, moves onto the global economic, academic, and innovation agenda.

4 The optimum role of government

Introduction

A common triple helix model of innovation is emerging in societies that previously held opposing conceptions of the appropriate role of government. In "high-state" societies, where triple helix relationships have traditionally been directed top-down, bottom-up initiatives appear in conjunction with the emergence of regions and the growth of civil society. In "low-state" societies with a laissez-faire tradition, the emergence of the triple helix is associated with a strengthening of the role of the state, acting together with university and industry, in shaping innovation initiatives.

The transition from industrial to post-industrial society has encouraged a shift in the role of government in both directions. Moving beyond Keynesian macroeconomic policies arising from the 1930s depression, such as central-bank adjustments of interest rates or money supply, is a difficult transition in the laissez-faire model of separate institutional spheres. In statist societies the transition of government from the total state, with central planning, to a more modest role of incentivizing innovation is a radical step. The traditional role of the state in innovation is most clearly apparent in countries such as Mexico, where state-sponsored industry sector associations and university consultative councils coordinate these spheres. The Singapore government organized the transition to high-tech manufacturing and then to knowledge-based economic development, the course and direction of which eventually became a matter of public debate.

Although a common mid-point can be discerned, the route to a relatively common triple helix of institutional equals differs significantly, depending upon the starting point of a statist or laissez-faire society. Different state capacities affect both the trajectory and the visibility of a triple helix, whether it is organized openly and transparently or is routed through hidden channels. This chapter discusses experiments in societies with "direct" and "indirect" innovation policies, aimed at achieving a common objective: knowledge-based economic and social development.

Direct innovation policy

Top-down models have been highly successful in organizing large military and space projects in both socialist and capitalist regimes. In countries with a planning system, government kept the entire innovation process under its control. Thus in the former Soviet Union and Eastern Europe, a system of research institutes focused on industry problems. However, the results could only be implemented if a central planning agency approved them. People from research and production units who knew each other sometimes made informal exceptions to the rule of centralized control. Although research and production were formally linked by intermediary organizations, industry's focus was on quantity production, not qualitative innovation and local technology transfer. Bureaucratic controls were an obstacle to the introduction of inventions but the more fundamental barrier to innovation was the disincentive to systemic change.

In the post-socialist era, top-down coordination was removed and each element in the former system was left to fend for itself, with sharply reduced funds from the state. Some research institutes obtained contracts from abroad; others tried to transform themselves into incubators and science parks. Many scientists and technologists left the country for positions abroad or stayed and tried their hand at new tasks, often in business areas unrelated to their former employment.

A few tried to start high-tech firms based on their knowledge and competency, often with the support of their institutes. Occasionally multinationals like General Electric, who invested in former state firms such as Tungsram in order to take advantage of skilled labor, also found stores of unutilized innovation that they could build upon. Nevertheless, the abrupt reconfiguration from a statist to a laissez-faire regime left a question mark where the state had formerly played a leading role.

Perhaps ironically, the state was assuming a greater role in innovation in other countries at virtually the same time as it was withdrawing from the scene in the former socialist countries. Concurrent with the Nokia success, which gave Finland the appearance of a country as an appendage of a corporation, government increased its role in innovation, making it a direct responsibility of the Prime Minister's Office. Finland was a much less technologically developed country than most of its Nordic peers in the early 1990s when the decision was taken to concentrate resources on science and technology in a few selected fields of IT and biotechnology.[1]

The monies gained from the privatization of public enterprises were utilized to raise sharply the level of public R & D funding. In relatively few years, the Helsinki region has become second only to Stockholm as a center of biomedical research in Scandinavia. Tampere, which had at most a few dozen IT researchers in the early 1990s, is now home to 3,000. The Finnish case suggests that the original premise of the linear model, concentrated R & D pump priming, is still valid.

Sweden is a more ambiguous case of conflicting policies in the context of relatively high R & D budgets. There was a substitution effect when a series of foundations, established with proceeds from the "wage earners' funds" to promote innovation, replaced funds cut from Research Council budgets. Sweden already had a high level of research funding and there was a feeling that there was inadequate take-up from existing research resources, so why spend more money?

Even though more money was not spent, there was a change in the way money was spent. The foundations encouraged a shift from disciplinary to interdisciplinary research, from small research groups to larger research teams, and to collaborative university–industry projects. There was also a dual dynamic of centralization and decentralization: concentrating resources at leading universities and spreading funds around to build up research at the regional colleges and new universities.

Devolution of the center

There has been a significant devolution of powers in recent years in countries such as Great Britain, France, and Sweden lacking a strong regional level of governance.[2] Formerly, central government operated through regional levels that mandated common policies and was a mechanism for carrying out these policies. Increasingly it is seen that it is necessary to have policies specific to the competencies and capacities of different areas. Moreover, it is difficult for a central government to mandate appropriate strategies from a distance. In Sweden some regions have been given a broader authority to develop their own regional development initiatives as an experiment. In Skåne, this has taken the form of projects such as the Medicon Valley Academy to foster the growth of a biotechnology industry and a functional food initiative. A recent idea is for a new PhD program, jointly initiated by the region and Lund University's medical faculty, and tied to industry.

Sweden uses the triple helix framework to knit together different initiatives at the national, regional, and local levels that might otherwise be at odds with each other. The model provides a rationale to cooperate and aggregate resources to a common end and reduce friction among what otherwise might be a set of small competitive initiatives. Different government agencies and foundations have established many innovation initiatives. Government has provided the universities with "holding companies" to transfer technology and help start new firms but it is only a modestly funded initiative. Technology bridge foundations were established in several regions with a significantly higher level of funding, for much the same purpose, and both collaborated and competed with the university efforts. Thus there are centrifugal forces dividing the various actors but there are also centripetal forces drawing them together to cooperate.

The central question in Swedish innovation policy is how to moderate the effect of centrifugal forces and increase the strength of centripetal forces. One clue to the trajectory for the emergence of the Swedish triple helix can be seen in the transfer of CONNECT, a local-level networking format, from San Diego to Sweden.[3] An initial attempt made by members of the local biotechnology association in Skåne did not succeed, lacking sufficient support from the region and the university. A later effort undertaken by the prestigious Academy of Engineering in Stockholm attracted support from regional officials and universities across Sweden—several CONNECT networks, linking entrepreneurs, business advice providers, patent lawyers, accountants, and angels, were successfully established.

Civil society and the triple helix

A triple helix coordinated entirely by the state provides only a limited source of ideas and initiatives. Under these circumstances government may take initiatives without consulting others; indeed it may subsume the other institutional spheres and direct their activities. Although large projects may be accomplished it is not the most productive form of triple helix relationships since ideas are coming from only one source, the central government; if the regional and local levels are active and there is input from universities and industry as well, then there is a much broader base to develop creative ideas for innovation as well as a better base for implementation, especially at the regional and local level.

A flourishing civil society of individuals and groups, freely organizing, debating, and taking initiatives, encourages diverse sources of innovation. The basis for a triple helix including bottom-up as well as top-down initiatives can be seen most clearly in countries that are just emerging from military dictatorships. The first academic revolution, the incorporation of research as a broad university mission, took place in Brazil in the 1970s, expanding the role of the university in society from a traditional support structure to one directly linked to national priorities. This transformation took place under a military regime where the university had relative autonomy. University discussion groups became a place where some internal opposition was tolerated even as many other academics were removed from their jobs and forced out of the country.

When the military gave up control in the early 1980s, a space opened up for university science and technology researchers to introduce the concept of the incubator from the US. At the same time a financial crisis led large-scale technology programs to be downsized, making smaller-scale initiatives, such as incubators to encourage the creation of start-ups, a necessity. At a later point, the national government built upon these programs and made them national policy. However, it was not until the re-creation of civil society that these local initiatives became possible. In succeeding years, various levels of government, as well as industry and civil associations, took up the incubator concept and spread it throughout Brazilian society, applying it to a variety of problems from raising the level of low-tech industry to creating jobs for the poor.

An incubator movement arose in Brazil, with local government supporting university actions and follow-on support coming from the national government, rather than being an isolated initiative as it is in Mexico. The Mexican government has a program to provide funds to universities to start incubators. However, it is a limited innovation mechanism with a very narrow base of support. It has not spread throughout the entire society whereas in Brazil, where the initiative was bottom-up and where various institutional spheres became involved, with the national government only one among several sources of support, the movement spread much more broadly.

Indirect industrial policy

An indirect and decentralized innovation policy, across the institutional spheres, may be more effective than traditional direct approaches since it is better able to take regional differences into account and incorporate bottom-up initiatives. Moreover, given the resistance to an enhanced role for the federal government, when intervention is decided upon it is typically carried out indirectly. The university was the institution of choice in three key instances: agriculture (mid-19th century), the military (World War II) and industry (the 1970s).

Although the industrial policy debate, and the conflicting visions of an active federal government and the idea that "the government that governs least, governs best," are as old as the US itself, the concept of industrial policy has to a much larger degree been forbidden in the US than in most other countries in the world. There is a high threshold to attaining government action to assist commercial innovation at the federal level. Various measures are typically held to represent nothing more than discrete answers to particular problems, such as the mid-1980s joint industry–government SEMATECH R & D consortia in response to the Japanese challenge to US dominance in semiconductor chips.

Government assumes a new role in innovation by encouraging university–industry interactions of various kinds. Government also plays a key role as public venture capitalist, through various programs at the state and federal levels to fill the gap between university support for firm-formation and take-up by angels and private venture capital. In a triple helix economy, firms collaborate to develop standards and new products, often with academic partners and government support.

This counterintuitive assessment of government's role in promoting high-tech industry in the US reflects the growing role of state governments in science-based economic development, as well as the federal government's programs to support technology development, especially in the defense and health areas in recent decades. Knowledge-based development represents a new initiative for state governments, beyond a relatively few like Massachusetts, that have been active for some decades. Virtually every state now has a science and technology (S & T) agency and at least one, and usually more than one, program that attempts to raise the level of S & T in the state and attract resources from elsewhere. Taken together, these programs represent approximately 3 billion dollars of spending per annum.[4]

State S & T policy is typically tailored to the industrial background and research intensity of the state. States with technology industries attempt to upgrade these industries by supporting local universities to work more closely with key firms, typically by supporting a research center that addresses some of the longer-range problems of these firms. Conversely, states without significant technology industries attempt to build research capacities related to a local natural resource in order to create a knowledge base that will enable them to take the next steps in firm-formation. Such a strategy may involve luring scholars with significant relevant research experience in these areas to the state by providing them with funds and other resources.

Enhancing an academic focus at a local university with possible future relevance to local economic development is now viewed as similar to traditional physical infrastructure development. States view these intellectual-capacity-building efforts as akin to building highways and bridges to improve transportation and encourage business. In the past state S & T efforts were typically funded through regular legislative appropriations, making them subject to cuts and even closure in an economic downturn. This was especially so because states, in contrast to the federal government, were required to maintain a balanced budget.

On the premise that intellectual infastructure is now as secure an investment as physical infrastructure, California has taken a new departure in state S & T policy with proposition 71, an initiative placed on the ballot and passed in the 2004 election. Formulated by a coalition of venture capitalists and disease-cure advocates, the measure will provide 3 billion dollars in debt financing through a bond issue. The funds will go to support stem-cell research at the state's public and private universities and to investments in biotechnology firms that are expected to realize the fruits of that research as marketable products.

It is expected that the borrowed monies will be paid back in the future out of the proceeds from intellectual property created from academic research and the equity generated in biotechnology firms. Federal programs that provide money to researchers and firms expect payback to government only indirectly and in the long term through increased tax revenues and job creation. The California initiative creates a direct link and feedback loop between university, industry, and government, seeking to create a virtuous circle of science-based economic development—Silicon Valley's next wave—based on public credit.

In a knowledge-based economy, characterized by increasing uncertainty due to the rapid pace of technological change, reliance on government policies that focus on supporting existing industries is no longer viable. Universities and other sites of advanced research are increasingly the seedbed of new economic development. Fostering the development of advanced research thus becomes the cornerstone of industrial policy. Picking future winners is an essential part of this process since resources spread across the board are never enough to accomplish a significant result. Once target areas of future growth are identified, based on judgments about present and future research capacities and market opportunities, the next step is to avoid the so-called innovation paradox of simply funding knowledge creation without an infrastructure in which to put it to use.

The foundations for new industrial development are then based upon the creation of organizational mechanisms, typically based on triple helix relations, to transform advanced research into economic activity. This new task increasingly supersedes the provision of physical infrastructure that is the traditional role of government in supporting industrial development, although the two are frequently tied together in transitional formats such as science park and science city projects. Government has an important role to play in an entrepreneurial high-tech economy, but industrial policy is now the immanent outcome of triple helix interactions, as in the California instance.

US innovation policy

As a result of strenuous opposition, there is reluctance to recognize that a plethora of specific policies and programs accumulated over more than a century constitutes a US innovation policy. Given resistance to government action at the federal level, when intervention is decided upon it typically occurs as a joint initiative of the federal and state governments, utilizing universities as an interface between government and industry. In response to ideological constraints, the trajectory of immanent industrial policy formation creates networks and initiatives that cut across the institutional spheres.

The development of university technology transfer capability served as an indirect industrial policy in a country precluded by laissez-faire ideology from taking an activist stance, in contrast to more direct approaches taken in Japan and Europe. However, the added value of bringing academia into closer contiguity to industry, through the creation of new firms from academic research, has drawn increased attention to this unintended consequence of academic technology transfer. Indeed, Africa, Asia, Europe, and Latin America increasingly hope to attain similar results from their universities by changing the rules of academic practice and offering incentives to academics to engage in activities that formerly would have been beyond the scope of the professor as "civil servant."

Government–university relations

Higher education is not a direct federal responsibility in the US, with a few notable exceptions: the military academies, Gallaudet University for the Deaf, and Howard University in Washington, DC, a historically black university. Nevertheless, the federal government has had a significant influence on university development by supporting the so-called agricultural and mechanical universities, the "land grant" schools oriented to practical subjects, with one-time subventions of federal lands as an endowment.

The funds provided for research pre-dated World War II but since they were primarily for agriculture they only affected a special sector of academia. Broad-based government funding of the universities was institutionalized in the aftermath of World War II, a conflict that had demonstrated the utility of universities as research providers and coordinators. Whereas the academic contribution during World War I had been largely limited to turning campuses into training facilities and providing researchers to work in government laboratories, World War II involved the universities more directly with the state.

The wartime triple helix

Despite barriers, a de facto innovation policy is created through pressures on government to act in crises. The World War II Office of Scientific Research and Development (OSRD), originated at the initiative of academic scientists, was active across the spectrum of research areas of potential military use. Under wartime conditions R & D, testing, manufacturing, and customer demand were integrated into "a seamless web," ignoring traditional boundaries.

Moreover, academics who had put aside their basic research interests to work as engineers on practical projects soon found that they had ideas for basic research that they would pursue after the war. This rediscovery of the connection between the practical and the theoretical, and the experience of working with virtually unlimited resources at their disposal, transformed the anti-government attitudes that had led academic scientists to refuse support in the depth of the depression.

The emergence of a peacetime R & D paradigm

Whereas close university–government ties were abandoned after World War I, they were institutionalized after World War II, albeit in a loose form so that control was limited and influence bidirectional, allowing universities, if they wished, to believe that nothing fundamental had changed. With the return of peace, universities and companies returned to their previous boundaries, with an important difference: the heritage of their wartime experience of cooperation and collaboration.

Prewar opposition to government funding of research at the universities was reversed as universities sought government funds. In addition to the precedent of ad hoc appropriations, a more systematic approach was developed through the establishment of agencies like the National Science Foundation, to disburse funds. Vannevar Bush's intention to locate both civilian and military research in a single unit was replaced by a plethora of research-funding agencies directed at special purposes.

On their part, the military solved the problem of obtaining useful results through close monitoring of projects supported in academia while maintaining a long-term perspective of what might be useful to the military and supporting research on computers and artificial intelligence. Although practical results from basic research were expected only in the long term, such results were the premise for the funding flow.

Provision of research funding was the basis for the continuing relationship and most of that funding went to research that government decided it needed. Nevertheless, the parameters, even of military research, were broad enough that basic research questions could be fitted within their guidelines.[5]

Research funders desired indeed the exploration of advanced ideas. For example, the US Army, in providing funds to explore development of an "autonomous land vehicle, also willingly paid for the establishment of new disciplines like artificial intelligence. The projects that PhD students worked on were "dual use." Thus a topic field such as a radio repair instruction manual provided valid problems for theoretical elucidation in expert systems. Nevertheless, while university–government relations flourished in the early postwar period, government–industry relations, while significant in the form of regulation and procurement, were not as thoroughgoing as the massive expansion of the research university system in the same period that was largely accomplished with federal funds.

Government–industry relations

A change in economic circumstances called for renewed attention to innovation. During the economic downturn of the 1970s there were proposals for government to become directly involved in aiding existing industries and building up new ones, but these were quickly defeated. Instead, government went through the universities to reach industry. The patent system was reorganized to give intellectual property rights from federally funded research to the universities, with the condition that they had to take steps to put them to use. After 1980 technology transfer mechanisms, which had been utilized by relatively few universities, were diffused throughout the research university system.[6]

Relatively little of the expenditure put into research was actually being translated into products, even given an extended time frame. To resolve this problem, the US created a public venture capital system as an extension of basic research.[7] It could not be called public venture capital but the National Science Foundation (NSF) program officers who founded the Small Business Innovation Research (SBIR) program recognized that a neutral terminology of stages and phases had to be utilized.

Extension from R & D to public venture capital: the SBIR program

In the beginning, the SBIR program was a minor-scale initiative in NSF, combining small-business support with funding for high-quality research and technology. The founding director of SBIR, in a personal interview, said,

> The starting point was that we saw a potential for economic development in cutting-edge research, but that there were no venture capital firms or others that were willing to take the risk of supporting activities with a very uncertain outcome. We were also interested in focusing on tomorrow's jobs, creating firms in tomorrow's businesses with international competitiveness.

SBIR thus expresses the growing awareness of technology as an important factor behind economic growth. Another important goal was to increase the return on investment of federal R & D. As its founding director stated, "hi-tech small firms seemed to be the best vehicle for doing that."

An intragovernmental initiative, including federal government research program managers, congressional staff members, and legislators, suggested that the SBIR should be extended to ten additional agencies, a proposition which was highly controversial in some circles. The universities and most people in NSF did not want it, neither did the national laboratories or the agencies themselves. All felt that this would take money away from current activities, although the amount of funds to set aside was less than 1 percent. However, the program was not controversial at all in political circles, and despite heavy lobbying against it, the Small Business Innovation Development Act (1982) was passed virtually without opposition.

The founder of the SBIR, in a personal interview, recalled that "because of the large opposition against the program, we had to choose our words very carefully, which contributed to making the program very good and bullet-proof." By describing, for example, a phase model of the entrepreneurship process and the role of the federal government in each phase, the SBIR created a neutral language for direct government intervention in the economy. That the act raised so little political controversy can also be explained by looking at the justifications for the SBIR. It was asserted that there was some kind of market failure because entrepreneurs with excellent but high-risk ideas could rarely find private funding. In addition, the strong focus on scientific and technical criteria provided a resemblance to (previously justified) basic research. Finally, "small business" can be viewed as a strong ideology by itself that very few people oppose. The originator of SBIR and similar initiatives, in a personal interview, said, "we definitely see the programs as a de facto industrial policy, but we cannot use that term, so we usually call it R & D policy and things like that instead; but it [SBIR] is a federal program that has created a whole lot of new industrial activity."

The expanded role of government in a laissez-faire society

Technology transfer from academia developed in several stages; perhaps the most important was the creation of a system of federally supported research in the universities. During the postwar period, high overhead payments became a method of funding the major research universities directly from the federal government, without explicitly accepting it as an explicit policy as is commonplace in Europe. These universities were clustered in relatively few parts of the country, on the East and West Coasts, with a few in the Midwest. This was not a major issue as long as academic institutions were primarily seen in their traditional role as educational and research institutions.

As new industrial areas arose from an academic research base in molecular biology and computer science in a few locations, other parts of the country became aware of the significance of universities as engines of economic development and wished to follow this model, first in North Carolina in the 1950s. In addition to creating their own S & T programs, states have become active proponents, along with their universities, of increases in federal R & D budgets. Indeed the salience of R & D spending to future economic development has spilled over from the budgets of the research agencies to so-called "porkbarrel" methods for funding local improvements through attachments made to other bills.

Given the realization of the connection between the location of research and the future location of industry arising from that research, pressure has increased on the federal government to increase research spending and to distribute it more broadly, eschewing peer-review mechanisms instituted in the early postwar period to focus federally funded research at a relatively small group of schools. Now that the connection of science and technology to economic growth is apparent, regions with low levels of federal R & D spending are unwilling to depend upon modest set-asides, instituted to reduce pressures for equalization, or to slowly build up their capabilities with local funds.

A science-and-technology policy has been developed that works the same way as appropriations for roads or bridges or any local improvement that a senator or congressperson wants for their district or state. A legislator typically attaches a provision for a research center for a local university to a funding bill for an agency with a related purpose, the so-called "earmark." The regular level of funding of these special bills is such that earmarks should be considered a regular feature of S & T policy, despite objections to the method.

Universities that have been outside of the research system but want to increase their research strength have also been active in seeking these funds. Typically, as this new group of research universities enhances their capabilities, through such targeted measures, they then begin to compete successfully for peer-reviewed funds through the normal research-funding channels. It is this increase in competition from universities across the country that has given the older research universities the feeling (indeed it is the reality) that competition for research funds has increased even as federal research budgets have risen significantly, especially in health and security.

The emergence of a "bottom-up planning system"

Although states can be explicit, the federal government can set only very general outlines in civilian innovation policy for fear that it will be accused of attempting to "pick winners." Government is ideologically perceived as naturally and inevitably incompetent, despite manifest success in military, health, and agricultural innovation. Nevertheless, it is advisable to watch what the US does rather than what it says with respect to government's role in innovation. Even the most conservative politicians are activists when it comes to creating new knowledge-based industry in their locality.

Since the federal government is precluded from playing a direct role in civilian technological innovation, it often seeds other institutions with ideas and develops them collaboratively. For example, Advanced Technology Program (ATP) officers regularly make visits to companies and hold national and regional conferences to encourage firms to work together with universities and government labs. Brainstorming sessions at these meetings typically include representatives of large and small companies, academics, and government technology experts.

The objective of the discussion is to reduce the general category of a critical technology to a particular point, at which the people who are closest to the technology agree that a blockage exists. White papers are encouraged around these strategic points and the funding competition is thus made much more specific. The result is a "bottom-up" planning process, an immanent triple helix arising across strong boundaries, with both top-down and bottom-up features.

Public/private partnerships

The growth of partnerships among small firms, between large and small firms, between large firms, and between firms of any size and university and government laboratories, often encouraged by government policies and programs, is increasingly common as an impetus to innovation. One such program in the United States was the Advanced Technology Program (ATP), founded in the late 1980s as a separate entity when it became too controversial to extend the operations of another body, the Defense Advanced Research Projects Agency, from military to civilian purposes. Another impetus was concern that the EU Framework Programs would encourage large US corporations to move significant portions of their research to Europe to take advantage of them. ATP consortia programs were expected to provide a counter-attractant.

However, the initial focus on large corporations was strongly attacked as corporate welfare, from both sides of the political spectrum. Moreover, ATP's direct interaction with industry was offensive to proponents of laissez-faire. More recently, as the ATP has emphasized interaction with industry, based on partnerships with universities, it has become somewhat more insulated to controversy by following the generally acceptable US "hidden-industrial-policy" model of focusing on small firms and university–industry interactions.

In its early years, the ATP operated primarily through a so-called "focused program" directed at a key industry problem. The ATP encouraged the development of infrastructural tools from the "bottom-up," encouraging companies to "brainstorm" ideas for collaborations at its regular conferences held in different parts of the country. This bottom-up approach has contributed to an environment where a more "natural" evolution of technologies has taken place from many piecemeal ideas that reflected the formative, summative, and "real-time" perspectives of a coherent program (in parallel with the development of standards).

The ATP has also acted as a catalyst in establishing collaborations, bringing together diverse firms and other organizations to pursue cross-disciplinary projects. For example, in the Health Information Initiative, healthcare providers, computer scientists, and information technology specialists participated in collaborative efforts. In several cases the collaborations that were formed included companies that under ordinary circumstances might never have worked together.

Although the ATP focuses on precompetitive research and emphasizes broad spillover benefits, small market-oriented firms tend to view their participation in ATP projects strictly in terms of competitiveness. They typically structure their projects to satisfy research requirements, on the one hand, and the firm's product development goals, on the other. Thus a "field deployment" to assess research results also serves as an alpha test site for an emergent product. Small research-oriented firms, on the other hand, tend to need nudging to remember the longer-term goals of product development. In both cases, the ATP experience tends to balance research and business goals.

The experience of firms in combining the research and business objectives suggests that while distinctions between precompetitive and competitive, and between research and product development, may be becoming less clear cut, this may be a positive development. It works toward promoting the competitiveness of US companies and achieving the ATP's broader goals of encouraging spillover among technological fields, enhancing the US innovation system. A key element of this system is a focus on firm-formation rather than renovation of existing firms, whether SMEs or large corporations, as was commonplace in Europe, until quite recently.

Beyond corporatism

Corporatism, the European doctrine of cooperation between government, industry, and labor, is superseded by a "triple helix" of academic–industry–government relations. A model of shared state authority is being transformed into one in which new forms of authority and legitimation arise from the bottom up as well as the top down. As a political model corporatism has had democratic and antidemocratic variants. In fascist formats such as Mussolini's Italy corporatism was a means of bringing industry and labor under the control of the state. Corporatism has also taken social democratic formats in which labor unions and employers' federations play a strong role in negotiating economic and social policy compromises with the state.[8]

Corporatist initiatives range from discreet, such as the New England Council in the 1930s, to the highly publicized brainstorming sessions held in the early 1990s, hosted by Joint Venture Silicon Valley, an industry-initiated group that included local government and university members. The emergence of a triple helix collaborative effort may also mark the entry of government into a new field facilitated through cooperation with partners. The new "quasi-public space" creates a regular forum for topics as yet of only peripheral interest to the general political process.

Although there is concern that the traditional public sphere is shrinking, a new quasi-public sphere of triple helix organizations is being created between representative government and private interests. Creating an organization or network, representing different interests, to build support for a regional focus is a key element in such strategy. The issues of knowledge-based economic development discussed in such quasi-public spaces are always subject to review by traditional democratic structures, such as courts and legislatures, should they become sufficiently controversial.

The debate over the future direction of research institutes through letters to the editor of the *Straits Times* in Singapore suggests the beginnings of the transition from top-down decision-making to open public debate. Correspondents questioned whether foreign research directors were developing research projects based on their personal interests rather than meeting Singapore's needs.[9]

The innovation state

The "innovation state" attempts to regenerate the sources of productivity in science and technology through new forms of cooperative relations. The basic precepts of an innovation state are set forth in a series of propositions about the transformation of traditional state functions to promote innovation:

1   Establishment of legitimate authority within a territory is extended from the public sphere to the private sector, promoting stability and reducing uncertainty in interaction.
    Corollary: government guarantees are given to private capital so that, with this insurance, it may take greater risks in investing in new ventures.
2   Levying of taxes to support protection of the nation and promotion of the general welfare is extended by using the tax system in a targeted fashion to provide special incentives and benefits.
    Corollary: R & D tax credits and reduced capital gains taxes are made available to promote innovation.
3   Establishment of rules to support economic life including laws to charter firms and foundations and to regulate the conduct of markets and currency systems.
    Corollary: new agencies are established to promote innovation, including hybrid public–private entities.
4   Use of legal system to establish special rights such as patents as temporary monopolies to promote innovation.
    Corollary: universities are granted control of intellectual property rights from government funded research (US, 1980; Denmark, 2000; Germany, 2002), incentivizing them to become involved in technology transfer and innovation. Universities in Sweden are subsidized through the holding-company initiative to encourage them to implement the third mission, beyond education and research, by contributing to economic and social development.
5   Provision of basic research funding to establish a linear model of innovation.
    Corollary: provision of public venture capital to create an assisted linear model of innovation.

Conclusion: the optimum role of government in innovation?

Science-and-technology policy was once the centerpiece of communist regimes legitimated by a thesis of a "scientific–technological revolution." After the collapse of communism and the discrediting of such government, it was difficult to justify more than a minimalist state, confined to basic security and welfare activities. Science-and-technology policy was barely a legitimate activity, no longer a priority in post-socialist countries such as Hungary. Thus science policy-makers and analysts sought a new conceptual framework for innovation to justify a role for government, and helped inspire the triple helix model.

A Swedish university liaison director, in a personal interview, once asked, "Why a triple helix; why not a 'double helix' of university–industry?" The answer is that it is only possible to develop university–industry relations up to a point, without considering the role of government. On the other hand, too much government control limits the source of initiative to a narrow range of officials. Finding the appropriate balance between too little and too much government has led to the creation of triple helix quasi-governance models in which actors from the three spheres, especially at the regional level, cooperatively create and implement policy initiatives.

The ideal triple helix configuration is one in which the three spheres interact and each takes the role of the others, with initiatives arising sideways as well as from bottom up and top down. Civil society is the foundation stone of the triple helix and of the relationship between science policy and democracy. Although a limited triple helix can exist under authoritarian conditions, a full triple helix occurs in a democratic society where initiatives can be freely formulated. As we shall see in the following chapter, the dynamics of innovation in a triple helix are typically worked out at the regional level.

5 Regional innovation

Introduction

The region is undergoing a fundamental transformation from a geographical, political, and cultural entity to a triple helix of firms, universities, and government agencies that generate new initiatives for regional innovation. The conditions for high-tech economic growth are not spontaneous creations; they can be identified and put in place by explicit measures.[1] The process of change may appear strange: it is neither solely market- nor policy-driven. In the initiation phase, science-based development typically arises from universities and other research institutions, acting together with either businesses or governments, or with both, around a specific focus. As the process takes off, new topics may be added to provide a broader base for regional development.

Regions such as Silicon Valley, Boston, and Linköping, Sweden, exemplify the trend toward firm-formation, rather than attracting existing firms to relocate, as a development strategy. These regions are distinguished by continuous firm-formation, a renewal process that transcends the particular technology that was its source. Indeed, the criterion for a successful knowledge-based region is the ability to move from one technological paradigm to another without a significant gap. The ecosystem supporting innovation and firm-formation becomes the driving force, with the ability to create and capture new technologies and business concepts as they emerge, and to draw them to the region.

As regions formulate knowledge-based innovation strategies, the constellations of actors, and their relative importance in the local political economy, are transformed. As entrepreneurial activities intensify, a cluster often takes on a life of its own that is no longer directly tied to a particular university or regional initiative. Successful regions may appear to be the result of a self-generating economic development process that is based on a lineage of firms. However, when the sources of regional success are analyzed, a university initiative and collaboration among triple helix actors can typically be identified. In the following we discuss the dynamics of knowledge-based regional development and the role of regional innovation organizers.

Toward a knowledge-based region

Regional identities are transformed as the traditional factors of production—land, labor, and capital—give way to knowledge in both high-technology and older manufacturing industries. A region is often an area of imprecise dimension that does not necessarily constitute a political entity but may operate with different types of political organization. These range from multifunctional governments, such as the German *Länder* and US states, to special-purpose districts for particular tasks such as transportation, pollution control, or business improvement. Quasi-political entities such as high-tech councils that lack official status may also perform government-like functions.

Regions were traditionally based on a natural feature such as New York harbor, the starting point for a global business and financial hub,[2] or the Tennessee Valley watershed, which became the setting for a hydraulic electrification and economic and social development scheme.[3] A regional identity may also emerge from a cluster of traditional firms—an Italian or Danish district with shoe or food products industries—or from new business concepts such as New York City's Silicon Alley multimedia firms.[4] New regional identities have been constructed through a "branding process" like the one based on the bridge linking the greater Copenhagen area in Denmark with southern Sweden. In this instance, Oresund is a new cross-border region with initiatives such as the Medicon Valley Academy to promote biotechnology.

Multinational entities such as the European Union encourage university–industry–government collaboration as a source of regional renewal and as a method of overcoming the barriers to regional development inherent in national boundaries. Cross-border regions, such as Oresund joining southern Sweden and Copenhagen, the Bothnian Arc where Luleå in Sweden and Oulu in Finland cooperate, and Cascadia linking Washington State and British Columbia, have been constructed by transcending inherited boundaries. The building blocks of these newly created regions include a source of knowledge, a consensus-building mechanism, and an innovation development project.

Regional triple helix spaces

Early 20th-century New England had knowledge spaces, research fields with technological and economic development potential at universities such as MIT and Harvard. The New England Council served as a consensus space where business, governmental, and academic leaders came together to test existing ideas, try out new ones, and develop an analysis that was appropriate to the region's problems and opportunities. Finally, an innovation space was created: an organizing effort for technological firm-formation that culminated in the invention of the venture capital firm.

A regional triple helix emerges from knowledge, consensus, and innovation spaces. A knowledge space provides the building blocks for regional growth in the form of a "critical mass," a concentration of research resources on a particular topic, from which technological ideas can be generated. When these resources reach a certain level, they may play a role in regional development. A consensus space denotes the process of getting relevant actors to work together: brainstorming, analyzing problems, and formulating plans. When these actors generate a strategy and bring together the resources to realize it, the regional development process can be moved forward. An innovation space denotes an organizational invention or adaptation made to fill a gap in the regional development process, often identified during the consensus phase. The organizing effort to create a new hybrid entity is similar to a social movement, bringing together resources, people, and networks across the triple helix.

Knowledge space

The initial stage is often the creation of a knowledge space consisting of a concentration of related R & D activities. Indeed, the availability of such a "critical mass" of research in a local area has been argued to be a necessary condition for science-based regional economic development. But it is certainly not a sufficient condition. US research universities supported by the growth of federal research funding during the post-World War II era constituted an enormous underutilized resource by the 1960s.[5] Faculty members who had worked with a few graduate students, with modest support, before the war, now led well-funded research groups that had access to increasingly sophisticated research instruments. Despite evidence of significant discoveries in the life sciences, only a relatively few successful instances of transfer occurred. Several of these universities later became the seedbed for significant regional economic development efforts while others are only just getting involved.

Research policy has been integrated with regional policy, whether directly as in Sweden or indirectly as in the US. Now that the role of academic research in creating new firms and jobs has been widely recognized, the concentration of national research resources at relatively few leading universities is no longer acceptable to other regions. In Sweden the Stockholm region was the major concentration, with additional concentrations in Gothenburg and Lund. The research council system of distributing funds primarily to the existing concentrations of research has been supplemented by two additional levels of research funding which have introduced regional criteria as one of the bases for distribution of funds.

The concept of "knowledge space" was first used to describe the decentralization of government research laboratories following the mid-1980s earthquake from Mexico City to other regions of Mexico where, inserted into new surroundings, they took on a new potential. The researchers began to think of how they could use their skills and the resources of the institute to address problems in their new locality. For example, a relocated agricultural institute took up the problems of the strawberry crop in their new locality. Then, more research institutes were relocated to give additional areas of the country the opportunity to create knowledge spaces. The decentralization of laboratories from Mexico City gave other Mexican regions a research capacity that had heretofore been lacking. These relocated research institutes still represent a potential for regional development that will be realized only if further steps are taken.[6]

Consensus space

A consensus space is a neutral ground where the different actors in a region, from different organizational backgrounds and perspectives, can come together to generate and gain acceptability and support for new ideas to promote economic and social development. From the analysis of the knowledge resources in a region awareness can be generated of their potential. Knowledge spaces are often transformed from potential to actual sources of economic and social development through projects originating out of discussions among participants whose backgrounds crosscut institutional boundaries. The very process of including actors from these various backgrounds in the strategy review and formulation process provides access to the resources required to implement the eventual plan.

In the late 1970s and early 1980s the Competitiveness Center of SRI International, a consulting firm that had spun out of Stanford University, advised Midwestern states, in industrial decline, how to organize regional cooperative groups to revive their economies. When the economic downturn affected Silicon Valley these policy researchers brought their model home and helped establish an organization, Joint Venture Silicon Valley (JVSV), bringing together high-tech company executives, local government officials and academics for a series of public meetings. Some ideas that came out of these discussions were then put into practice to develop new high-technology industries. One project, Smart Valley, for computer networks and information resources to help develop the next level of technology for the region, formalized some of the informal networks that have been found to be crucial to the development of high-tech industry in the region.

The classic example of a successful consensus space is the New England Council during the 1920s and 1930s where, in the course of a series of studies and discussions, the focus of regional innovation shifted from developing new products within existing firms to a strategy for forming new firms. Although the New England Council was limited to an elite, the meetings of the JVSV organization in the early 1990s were open to the public. The two groups had in common the ability to translate ideas into action.

On the other hand, the discussions held at the New York Academy of Sciences during the mid-1990s failed to attract industry and government representatives at a sufficiently high level to be able to initiate a viable action plan. Thus one problem in the creation of viable consensus space is the need to attract representatives from the different spheres with sufficient credibility and decision-making power not only to formulate a viable plan but to carry it forward.

In such discussions there is typically a debate between those who wish to initiate a project that can show results quickly and others with a long-term, larger-scale vision. For example, should the project meet the needs of existing firms or create the conditions for the development of new firms? This very issue was debated among formulators of the plan for the new branch campus of the State University of Rio de Janeiro at Friburgo. One group wanted to establish an engineering school that could supply BA graduates to work in existing firms. Another proposed the creation of an information technology PhD program to generate individuals with the skills to develop new technologies and, hopefully, new industries, and this idea was adopted.

There is a need to find a balance between projects that can demonstrate short-term results and large-scale projects that may initially be beyond the group's capability. Often there is a need to integrate disparate small initiatives and encourage collaboration rather than start entirely new projects. As these initiatives evolve, they typically include all the elements of the triple helix. Thus the State of Rio de Janeiro Industry Association took the lead in conceptualizing a plan for high-tech development in Niteroi, a city across the bay from the city of Rio de Janeiro. The association soon recruited representatives of the municipal government to the discussion. A consultant brought in to advise the process next introduced into the group faculty members and administrators from the Federal Fluminense University, located in the city.

There is often pressure to act quickly, to adapt a well-known mechanism such as a science park or venture capital firm, rather than to spend the time to carefully consider what is appropriate to a region given its state of development. For example, Accra, Ghana is at the very earliest stages of IT firm-formation. One policy entrepreneur wants to move directly into the innovation space with a proposal for the government to start a venture firm to support new technology enterprises. Another has suggested that rather than start a venture fund, the government should help, "bring Ghana's inexperienced IT people together. Let them talk. When people talk, ideas come up—and someone will pick up the ideas and run with them." [7] In this latter view, a consensus space is called for.

Innovation space

The innovation space may be visualized as a dual set of ladders with crossbars between them. One ladder is the linear model of innovation, starting from research; the other ladder is the reverse linear model of innovation, originating in societal needs. Crossbars between the ladders are represented by specific innovation mechanisms: incubator facilities, technology transfer offices, research centers, science parks, etc. Where the reverse linear side and the linear side meet, something unexpected that was not part of the original plan may result, such as an incubator with research-oriented firms and market-oriented firms interacting with each other.

An innovation space may start from the creation of a new organizational mechanism to jump-start knowledge-based regional development or it may proceed from the goals articulated in the consensus space. For example, in addition to providing a receptive venue for the concept of firm-formation from academia, the New England Council worked out an organizational strategy to realize that goal by inventing the venture capital firm. There is no single approach that is appropriate for all situations. An element that is present in one region may be absent in another and vice versa.

The basic phenomenon of science-based economic growth is generalizable but simply taking a mechanism that has been highly successful in one area and re-creating it in another may not work. For example, a region lacking a knowledge base with a critical mass may have built a science park simply expecting high-tech start-up firms to emerge, even without that sufficient knowledge base. Organizational mechanisms relevant to filling an innovation gap must be created. A more relevant strategy may have been to develop a research center on a topic with relevance to the region's economy, or even a university if one was lacking.

The best approach is to make an analysis of the strengths and weaknesses in a region and then design a development strategy. In 1930s New England this process identified a need for venture capital but the problem may differ in other regions. The missing link in the New York region is a lack of networks between the institutional spheres. In other regions, such as Oresund (Copenhagen, Denmark and southern Sweden), the analysis, calling for a physical link and symbolic focus, may differ yet again. This variation reinforces the importance of analyzing regional strengths, weaknesses, and opportunities before taking action.

Physical artifacts such as the Science Park at Stanford or the ring road around Boston are superficial after-the-fact characteristics, rather than an underlying cause of high-tech economic development. Knowledge-based regions like Silicon Valley and Route 128 are the cumulative result of interaction between governments at various levels, universities, and industries. Networks are generated from a variety of sources. For example, they may emanate from collaborations between large firms and academic researchers. When the Pharmacia Corporation left Uppsala, Sweden, many researchers remained. The ties that had earlier been created between the firms' researchers and their colleagues at Uppsala University then became the basis organizing biotechnology firms. An individual may also take the lead in bringing a group of firms in a field together to discuss common interests and undertake collaborations. This may lead to the organization of an association such as "radio valley" in Gothenburg, Sweden, or the effort to organize a photonics cluster in Recife, Brazil.

Triple helix spaces and science-based economic development

A summary of the phases of regional knowledge-based economic development can be found in Table 5.1.

The regional triple helix spaces are nonlinear; they can theoretically be created in any order, with any one of them used as the basis for the development of others. The process of enhancing regional innovation may start with the knowledge space, and move to the consensus space and then to the innovation space, in a linear fashion, or start from the consensus or innovation space and proceed from there. On the other hand, the process may start in the innovation space directly, with the development of a project or initiative. For example, an executive of the Downtown Partnership, a New York development agency that took an interest in promoting incubators, said that she could get the necessary information by "calling around"; an elaborate process was not necessary once her agency had made the decision to act. Some action is better than an endless discussion project and even an initiative taken in a vacuum can be improved, assuming it does not quickly fail and disappear. Other elements, like an effective discussion forum, may be added later to make the regional project more effective.

Table 5.1

Triple helix spaces	Characteristics
Creation of a knowledge space	Focus on collaboration among different actors to improve local conditions for innovation by concentrating related R & D activities and other relevant operations
Creation of a consensus space	Ideas and strategies are generated in a "triple helix" of multiple reciprocal relationships among institutional sectors (academic, public, private)
Creation of an innovation space	Attempts at realizing the goals articulated in the previous phase; establishing and/or attracting public and private venture capital (combination of capital, technical knowledge and business knowledge) is central

The regional space consists of the set of political organizations, industrial entities, and academic institutions that work together to improve the local conditions for innovation, forming the regional triple helix. These three key elements in the regional space play their specialized roles in a regional organizing process. However, if one element is missing, or constrained from participating, another may take its part. For example, if a regional government is lacking, a university may take the lead in encouraging firms to cooperate with universities or other knowledge-producing institutions. A collaborative culture, and the experience of different actors working together, provide a secure base for developing an innovation strategy.

The regional innovation organizer (RIO)

Who shall assume a leadership role in resolving innovation crises at the regional level is a frequently asked question even in countries with strong regional governments. At the regional level, in many countries, there may not be a governmental actor available to take the lead since there are no or only very weak regional governments. Portugal, for example, does not a have a strong tradition of regional government. In this situation the University of Aveiro took the lead in bringing together companies and municipalities, playing the role of innovation organizer. An organization that takes the lead in enunciating a development goal and coordinating cooperation among a group of organizations to carry it out is a regional innovation organizer. Since governmental boundaries often do not coincide with economic districts, there can be a leadership vacuum.

A company or a university that takes the lead in recruiting partners and managing the interaction among a group of firms in a region may fill this gap. Stanford University had to take the lead in order to create a technical industry surrounding the university. This process took decades. The firm-formation activity that was observed in Silicon Valley in the 1960s and 1970s resulted from initiatives dating to the end of the 19th century that encouraged students from the Stanford engineering school to form firms. It was realized that a great technological university required a support structure of firms. Otherwise graduates would move elsewhere and the university would remain a small isolated entity.

Such "greenfield" sites lacking previous development may require different strategies than "brownfield" sites with previous industrial development. Certainly the constellation of actors will be different, with previously industrialized areas typically having firms in a state of decline that may be too occupied with their own problems to support new firm-formation. Indeed, they may oppose it, wanting the resources to save their own companies. On the other hand, greenfield sites may lack actors with industrial experience. In the following case the university, as the major available organizational resource available, creatively adapted a state government program to local circumstances to stimulate firm-formation.

The university as regional innovation organizer

Exurban Long Island lacked an industrial base and local government was relatively weak. The most significant institutional actor in this far region of New York City, apart from a nearby federal laboratory, was a research campus of the State University of New York (SUNY). Expanding upon a single mode of technology transfer, the patenting and licensing of intellectual property, SUNY Stony Brook has taken the lead during the past two decades in formulating a knowledge-based regional economic development strategy, utilizing local, state, and federal resources.

The New York State science-and-technology policy of helping local industry through centers of advanced technology at local universities was not relevant to the Stony Brook campus of the State University of New York, located in a greenfield site in Suffolk County, 50 miles from New York City. The exurban site was selected to be nearby the Brookhaven National Laboratory, an asset for a science-based university. The campus was located beyond the zone of suburban industrial development, the exodus of industry from the city having halted well before Stony Brook. Given the lack of industrial development, Stony Brook developed a strategy similar to the one initiated just prior to World War II by Frederick Terman, then dean of engineering at Stanford University, in Santa Clara County, which at that time had similar characteristics to Suffolk County during the postwar era.

The presence of a medical school with extensive research capabilities in molecular biology suggested a focus on biotechnology. The technological area for selected start-ups was one in which the university had special strength. Former President John Marburger, stated in a personal interview, "We had a very clear concept of what could work . . . start-up companies in biotechnology." Moreover, a gap was identified in R & D and pilot plant facilities that the university could fill and thereby assist the development of biotechnology firms. Based upon the observation that such companies typically spend a considerable portion of their start-up capital equipping their laboratories and plants, if some necessary facilities were provided by the university it was thought that a Stony Brook "location would be more attractive to these companies." Providing firms with access to shared R & D infrastructure was matched by an effort to expand the research capacities of the faculty.

The university adapted an award from the New York State Centers Program to meet its special circumstances as a greenfield site. The Stony Brook Biotechnology Center ran what might be called a pre-Small Business Innovation Research (SBIR) program, directed at uncovering the commercial potential of research findings. For more than a decade, the center has offered funds to seed new faculty research projects that had some near-term commercialization potential. Typically, faculty utilized the funding program to take a basic research finding that had originated in their laboratory and examine it from a product-oriented perspective.

The center carved out a key role for itself in the campus technology transfer effort as a business, economic development and granting center. A professor present on the faculty, with previous success in organizing a biotechnology firm, provided a significant role model for his peers. Establishing an incubator facility was the next step in the university's regional development strategy of creating high-tech industry adjacent to the campus. Having both spheres available to work in tandem can be the basis for a further stage of mutual development, a coevolution of university and industry exemplified by the following case.

Entrepreneurs as regional innovation organizers

In the Linköping region of Sweden, a regional development initiative, originating in a firm, moved into the university. In contrast to Long Island, where the academic institution was the only available source of initiative, Linköping had an industrial actor, as well. A group of entrepreneurs have created high-tech firms in the region, encouraged directly or indirectly by Saab Aerospace. The linking element was provided by an industrial liaison officer, appointed by the university, who invited the local technical entrepreneurs to form a discussion group at the university. This entrepreneurs' club grew into a project to make university resources available to assist the development of the firms.

In a next step, an academic unit to train students as entrepreneurs, the Center for Innovation and Entrepreneurship, was established in order to encourage a firm-formation process from the university to complement the one that had already emerged from industry. Although many technical academics, especially in the engineering sciences, had formed companies, they typically functioned as individual consulting practices since professors were restrained by Swedish academic culture from pursuing the practical implications of their research in the direction of firm-formation. Students were not similarly restrained from firm-formation once an organizational path was opened up.

Student entrepreneurship, encouraged by incubator facilities, was then adopted by regional authorities who supported it as an economic development strategy. Large firms, downsizing their businesses, also contracted with the Center for Innovation and Entrepreneurship to train their employees, who were being laid off, in entrepreneurship and firm-formation. The model was transferred to other universities in Sweden and abroad. By utilizing entrepreneurship-training capabilities developed at Linköping, the teaching model could be introduced to other universities quickly. Instead of each school developing their own set of courses, they could draw upon a tested model. In the following case, a state government initiative with business support transformed the knowledge space by creating a critical mass of company and government R & D units that led to upgrading of area universities as well. This knowledge-based regional development process reshaped the identity of the region from low-tech to high-tech and shifted its image from a low-wage to a high-wage area, despite the reality that dual formats coexisted.

Government as Regional Innovation Organizer

The development of the Research Triangle Park in North Carolina was initiated in the 1950s by Governor Luther Hodges in cooperation with three area universities and the North Carolina business community. This prototypical example of the construction of a high-tech region by exerting regional political power at the national level resulted in significant national R & D resources moving to a less research-intensive region. The motivation for high-technology development was the desire to achieve a measure of economic diversification for a state economy narrowly based on tobacco and textiles. Land was obtained for a science park situated between the area's three major academic institutions. Relocation of federal research facilities to the region was an important factor in the park's eventual success.

The Research Triangle Park was the physical manifestation of a successful strategy to attract branch laboratories of federal agencies to the region. This research base was then used to attract smaller R & D laboratories of leading technology firms, such as IBM, to locate in the park. The establishment of an IBM research facility was a key event which led to takeoff. The state's three leading universities were the official locational points of the triangle but hardly the centerpiece of the state's development strategy. In the early years of realizing North Carolina's high-tech ambitions, the universities provided an intellectual and cultural ambiance, making the Research Triangle an attractive residential location for scientists and engineers.

Technology companies considering locating a branch in the south typically think of North Carolina first; its "critical mass" of federal and corporate labs gives it a competitive advantage in attracting additional organizations. Nor is the original North Carolina strategy easily replicable; opportunities to relocate major laboratories are rare. An important lesson from this initiative was that it took decades to successfully create a science park, undiluted by general industrial ventures. Less patient attempts in other regions gradually became general industrial parks as land was sold and leases were let for plants and professional offices. The park only recently became part of a firm-formation dynamic, instigated by firm closures.

The triple helix region

Route 128 and Silicon Valley have evolved a common model of science-based regional economic development, despite some cultural differences.

Continuity in the origins of the model of science-based regional development between Route 128 and Silicon Valley (MIT and Stanford) can
be discerned in the work of Vannevar Bush and Frederick Terman, who
were respectively a teacher and a student at MIT. The model of science-
based economic development from academia through the mechanism
of the venture capital firm was transplanted from MIT to Stanford in
the early postwar era. Some of the model was transferred as a result of
Terman's being around MIT during the war as director of the Radar
Counter-measures Lab at Harvard where he had the opportunity to ob-
serve MIT's mode of academic development.

In a 1943 letter to the treasurer of Stanford, Terman proposed an intensive replication of the MIT model in Northern California. Terman advised his friend

> what I have seen about the way that MIT operates in connection with
> industry, this is what we have to do as soon as the war is over. We
> have to form research centers, we have to establish firms. We must
> make this a central thrust of Stanford if we are to become a major
> university.[8]

The vision that Bush and others at MIT were working from goes back to
the ideas of William Barton Rogers. The founder of MIT wrote a report in
1846 propounding the idea of a university, not a technical school, which
would be involved in basic research and technological development.

Rogers' idea was that science would infuse industry, not merely with
low-level consulting from engineering design work but with longer-term
results of fundamental research. MIT always had a broader scheme of
education than merely technical subjects. The goal was to encourage its
graduates to take a broad view appropriate to an organizational leader
rather than a technical assistant. Thus MIT established a humanities department which was oriented to the technical areas. Similarly, when MIT
recruited physicists in the 1930s, it recruited the people who had an interest not only in basic research but in the utilization of results. Thus when
Van der Graaf was recruited from Princeton, MIT also arranged to have
his patent rights transferred from Princeton to MIT.

Some historians have interpreted the recruitment of basic researchers to MIT during the 1930s as a sign that MIT was moving toward the
general research university model in the US. Actually Karl Compton, the
president of MIT, was recruiting a particular subset of physicists, a subset
that had both goals in mind. The integration of academic and business
goals is the basis of the entrepreneurial university and knowledge-based
regional economic development. The industrial base emanating from a
university often retains some of its academic heritage. For example, the
biotechnology firms in the Boston and Bay areas, and elsewhere, have
a common quasi-academic mode of operation. Advertisements for post-

doctoral fellows to work in firm as well as academic laboratories can be found in *Science* and other journals. Common social networks that go back to college and graduate school are sometimes the source both for the business and the technical sides of these firms.

Saxenian (1994)[9] has emphasized discontinuities of organizational style between these two leading high-tech regions. The issue is structure versus network; vertical organization versus lack of hierarchy. On the one hand, Data General, an old-line minicomputer firm, had a flexible development group in its heyday. On the other hand, the later years of decline at DEC on Route 128 and the recent past of Hewlett Packard, a hierarchical operation in Palo Alto, may not be too dissimilar. As an observer noted, "Resource allocation (a focus on traditional bureaucratic procedures rather than unconventional ways of unleashing new ideas) is just as likely to hobble creativity in large and vibrant Silicon Valley companies as it is in boring, old industrial age companies."[10] The broader significance of this debate lies in the issue of whether these two regions represent unique historical instances or essentially common phenomena.

The implication of the "uniqueness" hypothesis is that if Silicon Valley and Route 128 were phenomena that arose in particular circumstances, then they may be replicable. The attempt in the UK to set up science parks may have been misguided or perhaps the process is often simply longer than many wish to accept. For example, when visitors came from Australia, the UK, and elsewhere to visit the science park at Stanford during the 1970s, the firm-formation process they were observing was already the result of 50 years or more of work. The park had originally been built as an industrial park, simply to earn more money for academic development at Stanford. However, the companies that wanted to locate in the park near the university were typically already closely related to the university. The guidelines for the park were soon revised to limit tenants to firms wishing to maintain university links. Thus the research park was born. The park was the end result, not the starting point, of a process of encouraging the creation of an organizational capacity and ethos to form firms around the university.[11]

Creating the regional triple helix

What are the necessary and sufficient conditions for creating a triple helix region, a knowledge-based conurbation that has the capability to renew itself across technological paradigms? The criteria for success are not only the ability to create a cluster of high-tech firms but the ability, over the longer term, to generate additional clusters as earlier successes are superseded. The transition from minicomputers to biotechnology in Boston exemplifies this process of knowledge-based regional renewal across technological paradigms. Cambridge, Massachusetts has recently been recognized as having the largest concentration of biotechnology activity in the

US, demonstrating that the region's early success with high-tech innovation in minicomputers was not a unique phenomenon.

A region with a broad-based entrepreneurial university has the capability to transcend a particular technological paradigm and renew itself through new technologies and firms generated from its academic base. An entrepreneurial university can be found either as the source of virtually any high-tech region or as a consequence of its development. Such a university should be broad enough in its focus to be at the forefront of several areas of advanced science and technology, only some of which have short-term potential for application. If a university is too narrowly focused, say on applied IT, as at Karlskronna, Ronneby, Sweden, the ability to develop alternative knowledge-based sources of economic development may not be available.

Triple helix regions may also emerge as the unintended consequences of policies designed for other purposes. For example, the recent emergence of northern Virginia as a technology region was both a result of its contiguity with the federal government and a consequence of the belief of many in government that it should decrease in size. On the one hand, the federal government promoted the "Star Wars" ballistic missile defense system which required advanced systems development capabilities and complex software. On the other hand, a conservative government wanted to eliminate programs as part of an effort to reduce the size of government. Nevertheless, it still wanted the results of the programs and thus adopted a privatization strategy, generating spin-offs from its laboratories.

A start-up process emerged in the Washington, DC area, formerly a one-industry region based on government, from government's increasing technology requirements. Firms formed to get government technology contracts wanted to stay close to their customers, the government agencies that were the source of their business. The enhancement of academic capabilities at George Mason University, and the development of a northern Virginia extension of the Virginia Polytechnic Institute in Blacksburg, arose as a consequence of this government–industry relationship. Northern Virginia is emerging as a triple helix region, led by the presence of government agencies that create a demand for high-tech products and help create a local industrial and academic base as a by-product.

Policy implications

Regions may be viewed as "thick" or "thin" depending upon the presence or absence of innovation support structures, whether informal or formal. Whether it is important for a region to create new organizational mechanisms thus depends upon whether firm-formation is already taking place, supported for example, by a network of angel investors, or requires a formal support structure, such as an incubator facility, to take off. A region that is rich in business development requisites such as venture capital and an entrepreneurial culture may not have to develop as many explicit organizational mechanisms as one where these are lacking.

Europe has announced the Lisbon Agenda, an ambitious goal of catching up and surpassing US science-based economic development by 2020. The "region" has assumed a special significance in this European Union (EU) plan that includes initiatives to develop concentrations of research strengths and bridging mechanisms like the US SBIR program. The EU is constrained by its charter to identify topics not well developed at the national level and the region meets the EU criteria of "additionality," adding value where nation states have been relatively inactive. Both declining industrial regions and areas lagging behind in development have been the focus of attention.

The traditional European innovation strategy has been the "learning region" based on incremental innovation, emphasizing close relations between firms and customers as the basis for innovation. Building upon existing assets rather than creating new ones is the basic strategy. Universities in a learning region can be expected to focus on traditional university–industry relations such as preparation of trained human capital and informal relationships such as consultation. Learning regions are more oriented to low-tech than to high-tech, to government–industry relations rather than to university–industry relations.

At the turn of the new century the US model of discontinuous innovation based on firm-formation surpassed the previous innovation fashion of incremental innovation in large firms, characteristic of Japanese corporations. Certainly, the two paradigms are not mutually exclusive. Indeed, the ultimate objective of initiating start-ups is to grow a reasonable number of these new firms to the scale where they can provide significant employment opportunities and productivity growth. How to create the conditions to generate a continuous start-up and growth process within and across regions is the fundamental issue.[12] University–industry–government collaborations, creating support structures for innovation, are the topic of our next chapter.

6 Triple helix technopolis

Research centers, technology transfer offices, and science parks, and the interaction among them, are emerging as the driving force of science-based economic and social development.[1] As these organizations grow and expand their capabilities, some of the tasks they undertake overlap those of their counterparts. A research center may develop an industrial liaison office. A technology transfer office that formerly licensed intellectual property to existing firms may also form new firms based on intellectual property generated at the university. The science park, originally intended to serve as a receiving point for successful firms generated from academic research, may also establish an incubator facility to start new companies.

The science park model comes full circle when a park founds a new university as a platform to encourage future spin-offs. Incubators may draw in firms from outside the university from parts of government laboratories, and from university research groups in order to incubate research centers as well as new firms. In addition to linking different disciplines within the university, centers also mediate between the institutional spheres by including industry representatives on their advisory boards. Technology transfer offices extend their internal and external capabilities, identifying potential research funding providers, as well as purchasers of academic technology.

The potential for collaboration is enhanced as university technology transfer offices, research centers, clusters, and science parks in a region become part of an interconnected web. The increasing interrelationships among the various innovation organizations encourage crossover between government and university and between university and industry. As the density of an innovation space increases, a series of relatively isolated innovation organizations may be synthesized into a self-sustaining regenerative source of economic and social development, a triple helix technopolis.

Convergence of innovation initiatives

There is a convergence under way among research centers, technology transfer offices, science parks, and clusters. As they develop, they remedy deficits in their functioning by incorporating elements of a counterpart in their organizational design. Thus a science park in an isolated location may find that it needs the generative force of an entrepreneurial university as a source of firm-formation. Conversely, a university seeking closer links to industry may establish a science park adjacent to its campus to provide a support structure for its research and training programs as the next step in its development.

A hybridization process takes place as various organizations integrate different innovation activities into their portfolio, filling gaps in the knowledge, consensus, and innovation spaces. Instead of technology push and market pull operating side by side with industrial clusters, and university research groups operating separately, they are linked directly or through intermediaries. For example, centers organized by academics often include firms as members. Science parks may provide a home for university departments as well as companies. Low-tech clusters increasingly find that they require a higher increment of knowledge. Building a university, in addition to a vocational training school, may be the next step in the upgrading and development of a cluster.

University technology transfer offices interact with industry to translate embryonic technologies from academic to industrial formats. Such offices produce transaction benefits such as the added value that arises, on the one hand, from encouraging academic inventors to be involved in developing the implications of their technology and, on the other, from arranging for additional development work by industrial customers. The transfer office also provides a search mechanism to identify potential users of knowledge who may not already be in the informal network of university–industry relations or even within the circle of scientific journal readers.

An appropriate legal infrastructure for university–industry relations is required to realize additional benefits from a knowledge space. Government has created innovative formats for the protection of intellectual property that have spread from industry to academia. Patents publicize inventions, making protected knowledge available as a public resource for others to create new knowledge. This new knowledge can itself be privatized and protected even as it is also publicized, creating a continuing steam of invention and innovation.

The emergence of the technology transfer office

An initial step toward the entrepreneurial university is often the creation of a technology transfer office as an internal search mechanism to identify commercializable technology and as an external search mechanism to identify potential customers. This development in academia is paralleled by the establishment of similar intelligence and transfer capacities within the firm. Such units identify technology developed within the firm that may be utilized in other parts of the company or marketed outside, as well as identify technology that it needs to import.

Early postwar funding of research was justified on the basis of an endless-frontier metaphor with an assumption that research results would flow easily to industry in the form of publications. Government was precluded from taking steps to develop technology itself except in strictly limited areas mostly related to national security. Wartime experience had clearly shown the need for enhanced interaction between university and industry, in order to quickly provide useful technology to the military. Since time pressures were not expected to be as great in peacetime, the presumption arose that a more relaxed technology transfer mode, such as that provided by publication, could suffice.

After a few decades and several billions of dollars of research funding, questions began to be raised about the efficacy of this approach and studies were commissioned in the late 1960s to investigate the issue.[2] With few results of university research turning into products outside of the military area, agencies sponsoring research hired patent officers to manage the government's intellectual property. They began to work closely with their counterparts at the very few universities that had technology transfer offices during the early postwar period. Given an increased interest in seeing intellectual property put to use, government patent officials developed administrative procedures to transfer intellectual property to universities interested in commercializing research. This was a stopgap measure but one that began a trend.

The issue of university intellectual property initially arose in the context of government funding military research at universities during World War II. It was realized that such research would produce useful results beyond immediate war needs and that these intellectual property rights should be protected. However, what was not decided at the time, or necessary given the immediate focus on developing technology to win the war, was how those rights should eventually be utilized. When it was decided that the federal government should continue to fund university research after the war the issue of disposition of intellectual property rights was not clarified.

The public-interest issues arising from the resources created with taxpayer funds, on the one hand, and the private interests of the inventors and potential industrial users of these results, on the other, were debated in Congress and elsewhere but were not settled until the industrial crisis of the 1970s brought these issues to a head. The Bayh-Dole Act of 1980 resolved the contradiction between the government ownership of intellectual property rights in the research that it funded at universities and the wish to see those rights put to use.

The Bayh-Dole regime took into account the need to incentivize all participants to advance commercialization and maximize access to knowledge created with government funds at one and the same time. While university technology transfer pre-dates Bayh-Dole and was on an upward trajectory at the time of its passage, the act codified and legitimized a set of informal practices and relationships that had emerged between university, industry, and government during the preceding century.

Technology transfer offices view the Bayh-Dole Act as the charter document of their profession. Indeed, some have analogized it as the "Magna Carta" of academic technology transfer. The act provided the impetus for virtually all research universities to become involved in technology transfer, beyond the few that had early identified it as a significant task.

Moreover, the act opens the way to creation of a new funding stream for academia from the proceeds of technology transfer. Some universities have extended the scope of the Bayh-Dole regime through internal rule-making, and claim rights over all intellectual property resulting from university research on the grounds that the intellectual and social atmosphere of the campus is an essential ingredient to faculty invention. The Bayh-Dole Act and technology transfer offices improve efficiency in the technology transfer process by clarifying individual and organizational roles and by providing guidelines for the sharing of financial rewards.

Issues of intellectual property rights at the university–industry interface have not yet been clearly addressed in Mexico, where there is also a problem of weak enforcement of patent laws. This has had the effect, on the one hand, of firms tending to rely on secrecy as their primary mode of intellectual property protection and, on the other, of requiring academics to turn over all intellectual property rights to the company and to refrain from publishing as a condition of research contracts. Secrecy is thus increased and university–industry interaction is limited due to a lack of creative compromise. Even though government takes steps to incentivize both sides to cooperate, stasis predominates in the absence of governmental action to provide rules of the game that balance the interests of academia and industry.

The technology transfer office as "innovation systems integrator"

The technology transfer office serves as an "innovation systems integrator" between university, industry, and government, bringing together various disparate elements to fill gaps in the technology transfer process. For example, when patentability was established, there was often a lack of means to demonstrate "proof of concept" to potential industrial partners. In the absence of other ways to show the validity of a technology idea, transfer offices adopted a firm-formation strategy.

Establishment of a feedback loop from the third mission of contribution to society to the first mission of teaching and the second of research occurred as an unintended consequence of carrying out the third mission. Thus technology transfer offices began to contribute to the research mission by helping researchers identify additional resources to explore the practical implications of their findings. Transfer offices also took on an educational role, in order to give faculty and graduate students a better idea of how to recognize a patentable invention.

Organizational capacities of the transfer office and university culture are essential ingredients of success. Indeed, these elements may be more important to technology transfer success than the nuances of a particular intellectual property regime. In the past, patents and licenses were largely by-products of high-quality basic research. Patents that result in economic benefits are now increasingly sought after as direct outcomes, along with theoretical advance. It is the serendipitous result of basic research that is believed to have the greatest financial potential; therefore to induce researchers to focus on short-term projects would be counterproductive to the business objective of the office.

Technology transfer offices view themselves as part of the service mission of the university to provide public benefits by putting research to use. Even as the business arm of the university, transfer offices view themselves as promoting core academic values such as dissemination of knowledge through publication and expansion of research. Earning money is important, especially to reach the break-even point of earning enough to pay for the costs of the office and justify its efficacy to the administration.

Financial goals rarely predominate; most offices see their role as providing a range of services to assist their clients and view profit maximization from technology transfer as one objective to be balanced against assisting academics to put their technology to use, even when the financial rewards are not large. As one technology transfer officer said in reply to a query about return on investment (ROI), "Financial ROI is only one aspect [and often not stronger than other key aspects] that drives most academic institutions' tech transfer offices."[3] As technology transfer offices secure their financial base, they are more easily able to operate within a long-range time frame and undertake projects that do not have immediate marketability.

Academic inventors' publications and their interaction with scientists in industry help technology transfer offices identify commercial opportunities. Dissemination of research findings through publication may also help identify potential industrial partners and persuade them to provide gap funding that will move the findings toward utilization. Offices rely on their university's reputation and scientific strength to sell patents and identify partners for firm-formation. The necessity of aligning publication and patent time frames provides an incentive to make timely decisions in the "triage" process of judging commercial potential.

Once that potential is seen and protected, publication is seen by the office as an "advertising" mechanism to help identify potential licensees, especially among offices that are taking a longer-range view and patenting without having identified a licensee in advance. The ability to file provisional patents quickly reduces, if it does not eliminate, the potential conflict between publication and patenting. The cost of protection for an initial year when commercial potential can be assessed, before having to commit to the full patent process, has been made easily affordable.

At a few universities, the contribution of the office to research funding is already greater than the 8 percent average of industry contribution to academic research. A few technology transfer offices with a long-range perspective posit that revenues from technology transfer, especially from equity in successful firms spun out from the university, could make academia at least partially self-sufficient within the extended time frame of 50 to 100 years. By providing the universities with a virtual "land grant" of intellectual property, the Bayh-Dole Act of 1980 may eventually be recognized as the equivalent of the Morill Act of 1862.

Organizing the consulting relationship between university and industry

Many universities, especially in developing countries, are in the process of building research resources but are not yet able to capitalize knowledge through transfer. The increase in scale and scope of consultation provides a mechanism to "bootstrap" academic capital formation through a unit that that has the ability to identify and carry out larger projects than could be taken on individually. In this model, the consulting organization is an arm of the academic unit or department and thus returns profits to that unit. Alternatively, the consulting firm may move outside of the university and become an independent business, hiring individual scholars for specific projects or paying them retainers for exclusive availability to the firm. The internalized consulting model is exemplified by the CESAR unit at the University of Recife, Brazil, during the past decade or so, while the Arthur D. Little firm, spun off from MIT in the late 19th century, represents the classic externalized consulting model.

A service organization may be created, utilizing the human capital resources of the university to identify technological needs in industry or government and provide solutions. This unit is based on organizing the knowledge resident within the university and marketing the skills of faculty and students. It provides a professional capacity to seek external work, and puts together temporary groups of academics to provide the solutions, thus translating consulting from an informal individual activity into an organized group practice. One of the founders of an academic consulting unit described how, in contrast to a technology transfer office, "we work the other way around looking for problems that can be solved with human capital . . . One of the early jobs we had was a contract to develop the website of a large supermarket chain."[4] The earnings from these contracts provided the means to support academic development of the computer science department at the University of Recife. Consulting organizations and transfer offices, as highly organized formats for external relations, parallel the internal reorganization of research from a simple dyad of professor and student, or even research group, to a more intricate and focused organizational design.

The rise of centers

The trend toward center-formation originated in the experience of scientists and engineers working on joint projects during World War II who wished to continue the interdisciplinary collaboration they had found so exciting in wartime research and apply it to new goals such as expanding academic research capabilities and cooperating with industry. A university center typically brings together several research groups around a common theme for several interrelated purposes:

1   to attract a greater amount of funding that any single group could hope to attain;
2   to build a new physical facility or acquire an expensive research instrument; and
3   to undertake larger-scale research projects.

A center may bring together various intellectual, physical, and organizational resources within a single university or it may span several universities and non-academic institutions such as government research institutes and firm laboratories, whether in a local region or among several regions, to engage in more intense collaboration.[5]

The growth of centers is making the university a more complex organization, with faculty performing multiple roles in departments, centers, and technology transfer offices. Center directors increasingly resemble a corporate chief executive officer (CEO), administering the center and serving as a liaison with academia, industry, government, and the public. The formation of centers, bringing together diverse perspectives, expands upon the social process of research that takes place in scientific meetings, editorial board discussions, and conference planning groups.

Centers are typically based on the research mission of the university, although they increasingly include responsibility for outreach and public understanding of science. Although individual investigator grants remain a sacred tenet of US academic science, the National Science Foundation (NSF) and other granting agencies have made funds available on a larger scale to achieve various purposes. These include reorienting engineering schools from a theoretical and scientific to a more practical industry direction and encouraging the recruitment of women and minorities into scientific and engineering careers. Engineering research centers are expected to meet these broader objectives, and are provided with funds for this purpose, as well as their technology mission.

In an academic system based on departments and disciplines, centers foster interdisciplinarity by coordinating researchers within and across intellectual and administrative boundaries. Centers can also bring together university researchers with those from industrial and governmental laboratories. They allow the issues of non-academic organizations to be addressed in an academic format by scientists from each sector. In principle, centers are temporary bodies that may close if funds run out, whereas departments are part of the permanent university budget.

The formation of centers has become a tactic in an academic struggle for funds. In an earlier era large scale government funded centers were primarily located at major universities. More recently, establishment of a center has become a means for an aspiring university to move up the academic ladder. As a faculty member at a leading university explained in a personal interview, "The centers are our way of getting a lot of research support . . . But this has changed, centers are giving other universities . . . a mechanism which we've been using all these years . . . Now because NSF spreads the wealth, . . . it's the major institutions that are losing out." The formation of centers focuses faculty and resources around a common theme to create a critical mass of high-level research activity in a university previously lacking this attribute. However, most NSF engineering and science centers are still located at the major research universities. Nevertheless, to its surprise, MIT lost a competition for a research center to a coalition of second-rank universities a few years ago.

The center format is extensively utilized by state and local governments in less research-intensive regions as a means to develop concentrations of research relevant to their present and future economies. Centers also provide a neutral ground for company researchers to collaborate. The work done at the university is open, but the follow-up at the company laboratory can be proprietary. Centers enable companies to access the intellectual life in a university in "real time," eliminating the lag between research discovery and publication. A center director noted in a personal interview that

> if a professor is very interested in rapid processing, then [people in industry] will work with this faculty member because that is the main topic of his students' research. So they share an office and they work very close together so that the person [from industry] gets to know all the facets and you are constantly in touch with your company . . . It would be a means to incorporate new technologies much sooner and much faster.

Companies involved in this center wish to gain a competitive advantage by cutting the usual time it takes to learn about new research.

The precise limits of communication between firms and universities can only be worked out in practice. As one academic noted, "It is never clear where to draw the line. Some people will tell you more than others." A company scientist observed in a personal interview

> Everybody is willing to contribute to discussions if they feel like they are getting approximately equal in return. So if you get a person from a very restricted company . . . and you want to share with them but every time you say something you get back the answer from them like, "well, no, I cannot tell you that." After a while, you cut back on your interaction with them . . . and you operate on the principle of equality.

Over time, a norm of reciprocity emerges.

New forms of collaboration are invented as traditional informal modes of sharing information and credit are transformed into formal large-scale cooperation between researchers and their industry and government sponsors. Centers combine some of the lateral features of a strategic alliance among companies with the hierarchical characteristics of a traditional European professorship or research institute. A center is a succession of strategic alliances to achieve a longer-term goal. Part of that longer-term goal is usually the creation or enhancement of an industrial cluster connected to the centers' research. Such science-based clusters and their member firms often find it useful to maintain physical proximity to a university.

Renewal of the science park

The science park originated as a repository for firms generated by the university which wished to maintain the umbilical cord between university and firm. A science park is basically a real-estate development, ideally located next to a university. Its purpose is to house two types of research-oriented firms: companies that have grown out of the university and wish to maintain close ties, and firms that wish to locate an R & D unit, or even their entire laboratory, to a quasi-academic site. These latter firms often wish to pursue multiple objectives, including closer collaboration with academic researchers and the ability to invite potential recruitment candidates to work part-time in the firm before making a hiring decision.

The classic science park at Stanford University was the result of a decades-long process of firm-formation from the university.[6] Later science parks, often located near universities without an entrepreneurial orientation, were expected to encourage, or at least be a source of, firm-formation activities. Many subsequent science parks, typically built at isolated sites, have not been closely connected to academic centers, but have been home to multinational corporations and R & D units of national corporations. Even when they were apparently successful, like Kista Science Park in Stockholm (home to Ericsson R & D), they typically lacked the firm-formation orientation.

Although firm-formation is certainly an integral part of the stated purpose of most parks, few achieve this goal except as an unintended consequence of the departure of tenants, whose former employees may start a firm and remain in the area. For many years science parks provided primarily a place for large firms to locate R & D units, and secondarily a means to collaborate with academic researchers and recruit promising students. Science parks are currently being reformulated into multipurpose entities, taking on new tasks such as organizing new universities and incubating firms.

Introducing the forward linear model into a science park

Sophia Antipolis, near the French Riviera, is the closest European counterpart to North Carolina's "Research Triangle," emphasizing climate, contiguity to an airport, and inexpensive land as attractors. The plan for Sophia Antipolis was based on attracting existing labs and companies to relocate to a facility where they could be neighbors with their counterparts in four technological areas. Pierre Lafittte, the founder of Sophia Antipolis, also envisioned his park as a modern version of the medieval Parisian Latin Quarter, attracting scientists, engineers, businesspeople, and artists to a newly created suburban environment.[7] Indeed, Sophia Antipolis has theaters and arts festivals as well as space for its main clients—branch laboratories of multinational firms such as Glaxo-Welcome, the former Digital Equipment Corporation, and Rhone Poulenc, as well as French government-supported research institutes and some of the engineering and science faculties of the University of Nice.

Sophia Antipolis is a governmental initiative to encourage regional development and decentralization of research resources from Paris. It is similar to the Research Triangle Park in the US, except that the impetus comes from the political center rather than the regional level. Interaction with a university has been less important to its success than the ability to sell itself as an attractive location, a credible alternative to Paris, which is still the most common location for R & D in France. In an informal talk to visitors from a NATO Science Policy Workshop meeting in Nice, Lafitte indicated that in the future the emergence of multi-media software using content from the humanities and social sciences will make possible the realization of a missing element in his original dream of Sophia Antipolis as a "Latin Quarter" with a university in which all the academic disciplines will be represented.

Originating as an attractive location for existing entities, Sophia Antipolis has since acquired some of the start-up capabilities of Silicon Valley and Route 128, through necessity. Merger of multinational firms has made some laboratories redundant and subject to closure. In one instance a choice between a London and a Sophia facility was made in favor of the former. Nevertheless, with assistance from the merged firm, employees were encouraged to begin new firms; these soon equaled the employment of the old lab. At least two such closures have sparked a firm-formation effort which also brought in replacements for the old tenants.

Building a science park on the reverse linear model

The original concept of the science park as a destination point for firms formed from university-originated technology has been turned on its head. The science park has become a means to promote decentralization of research facilities. Universities without an internal dynamic of firm-formation have also used the format as a means to attract technology based industry to locate adjacent to the university to encourage interaction, or at least create an image of industrial relevance. The University of Colorado at Boulder made the transition from a teaching to a research university in the 1960s, supported by National Science Foundation program to develop a second tier of research universities. Along with the University of Utah, Boulder was among the leading candidates for academic distinction in the Rocky Mountains region.

As the local region in which the university was located suffered an economic decline and in accord with the efforts of other universities to gain support for research from industry, the university embarked on a plan to use vacant land adjacent to its campus to develop a research park. During the 1980s a plan to establish a science park encountered serious setbacks before it became successful. A university administrator had participated in the meetings of a national commercial real-estate association which, as academic interest grew, spun off an independent Association of University Related Research Parks. Through this group, the administrator learned about the experiences of other universities that had already organized parks and made contact with experts who could help the university develop its own project. A feasibility study was contracted to develop the physical plans and location site for the projected research park. However, the idea was shelved by the university's governing board when a trustee, with a background in real estate, pointed out that a necessary marketing and financial study had not been done.

A few years later a new administration received a mandate from the governing board to develop a research park. By the mid-1980s sufficient universities were involved in real-estate development to support both a professional association of university administrators involved with the issue and specialized consulting firms to assist them. In addition to obtaining the necessary outside expertise the administrator also made an effort to gain campus support for the project by establishing a faculty advisory committee. Between the consultants and the advisory committee, policies were worked out that, it was hoped, would make the project compatible with academic objectives and financially successful at the same time.

For example, it was decided that the research park would only attempt to attract firms in areas in which the university already had or could reasonably expect to acquire significant research strengths. A prime academic goal for the park was thus increasing the number of scientists in the region in fields in which the university had strength or might want to develop strength. This would provide consulting opportunities for faculty, jobs for graduates, the possibility of joint research projects, and industry funding for academic research. A financial goal was the purchase, with projected research park profits, of additional lands for future university expansion. An enticement for the humanities disciplines that were not directly included in the project was the possibility of an off-campus institute partially financed with park profits but expected to raise most of its own support from foundations or other donors.

The plan was considered an immediate success when a regional telecommunications corporation decided to locate its R & D facility at the projected park. With the prestige of association with a major firm, it was expected that additional electronic technology firms would locate there. It was thought that in the long term the park would enhance the university's research capacities by supplementing inadequate levels of state funding while contributing to regional economic development. However, even when sponsored by a university and connected to it through a variety of research connections and financial arrangements, a research park is basically an independent entity set apart from the academic enterprise.

The gap between science park ideology and reality

The science park as a stand-alone suburban model works relatively well for self-sufficient units of large firms. They interact primarily with other units within their firm and with a university if the science park is located adjacent to one. Volvo and similar firms are the major tenants of the Chalmers University Science Park in Gothenburg, Sweden. The park location makes it convenient for a Volvo R & D unit to attract Chalmers students to work on projects in the lab, giving them a taste of industrial R & D, and to judge the ability of potential future employees without having to make an employment commitment.

Volvo has the opportunity to collaborate with university researchers by providing consulting opportunities for faculty members without disturbing the traditional organizational structure of the university. However, new technology-based firms have mostly located in downtown Gothenburg, to take advantage of lower rents and of the amenities of the urban infrastructure, like cafés. The relative absence of start-ups in science parks in contrast to the stated objectives of many such parks, has become the basis of an academic critique of their performance, calling into question the validity of the science park concept.

If the concept of the isolated R & D unit is outmoded, then the stand-alone science park is also obsolete. Similarly, the traditional cluster of a group of related firms, perhaps supported by a vocational training institution, is also outmoded and needs to be enhanced by a research component. Although education and research can be conducted separately, in institutes and colleges, a science-based entrepreneurial university fills both needs at one and the same time and also provides a strategic player with the capacity to take a long-term view of the region's future. One way to revise a science park from a linear or reverse linear to an interactive mode is to insert it into a vibrant urban environment.

A suburban-style science park is less suitable for new, small, high-tech firms than for the R & D units of large corporations. A relatively isolated location is an impediment to firms that want to be in close touch with each other and require a support structure that larger firms can afford to internalize. An urban environment provides easy access to a variety of supplies and services that even a large park can only partially duplicate. When there are fewer resources available this is an even greater problem. Thus in Recife, Brazil, few firms moved to a science park, built according to the classic model, located on the outskirts of the city.

Eventually a concept for an urban science park, Porto Digital, was created that would take advantage of and enhance an older urban infrastructure and make it hospitable for a cluster of high-tech firms. The founders of Recife's Porto Digital Science Park are renovating small commercial buildings on an island which was the historic city center and is now also the site of a reviving cultural center with cafés, restaurants, and historic buildings.[8] A key part of the project is moving the university's computer science department, a leading research center, to the science park, to be followed by the computer science departments of other area universities. While this will theoretically remove them from easy interaction with other disciplines, the gain in interaction with other computer scientists and IT firms is expected to outweigh this loss, given the strength of disciplinary boundaries.

Not any old urban infrastructure will do. The Yale Science Park, located in a group of abandoned factories in a declining neighborhood of New Haven, Connecticut, is as isolated a setting as any suburban park. However, the university and the city have recently committed to enhancing the surroundings of the park. Similarly, the Audubon Park, adjacent to the Columbia University Medical School in upper Manhattan, has had difficulty attracting biotechnology firms that, if they could stay in the city, preferred to locate downtown in a neighborhood with vibrant arts and cultural amenities such as Chelsea in lower Manhattan.

The science park university

The renewal of the science park is typically accomplished by introducing an academic element. The objective is to turn the science park into a generator of new firms by creating an entrepreneurial university. The change in direction is often the result of a crisis caused by the departure of a major tenant. For example, when Ericsson closed its chip-manufacturing facility at Stockholm's Kista Science Park, the viability of the park was in question. Park management revised its strategy and introduced urban elements of apartment housing units and shopping centers into the isolated suburban location. They also transformed a small branch of the Royal Technological University into an independent school, Kista Information Technology University, that includes an entrepreneurial training program and an incubator facility.

One reason for a science park to found a university is to introduce a firm-formation dynamic into the park. Science parks that simply provided a prestigious corporate location have found that they do not make a sufficient contribution to economic development when a systematic firm-formation process is lacking. The Porto Digital and Kista development projects merge the science park, cluster, and entrepreneurial university concepts into a larger whole. If the projects are successful, a self reinforcing dynamic of innovation will be created.

Governance in the triple helix

To carry out these projects, the science park management expands its capabilities from real-estate administrator to innovation organizer. The long-term goal is to transform the science park into a cluster with a mix of firms of different scale and scope so that innovation will take place through interchange and collaboration among companies. The introduction of an academic setting provides a neutral site for collaboration among firms, for example for center organization with academic researchers. There is also the potential to induce a firm-formation dynamic from academic research or jointly through interaction with the firms in the park, typically through a science park incubator facility. A new unit, such as the Electrum Foundation at Kista, may be created to realize these broader objectives.

Such a unit within the park is similar to organizations established to encourage innovation across broader organizational landscapes where universities, for example, may not yet be cooperating with each other. For example, in Monterrey, Mexico, at the initiative of the state government, public and private universities have established several cooperation initiatives preparatory to the development of a science park. A governance structure for the triple helix may be created to assist this transition in the form of a high-tech council. Such organizations play an initiating and coordinating role in a locality or region, bringing together existing resources and attracting or creating new ones.

Conclusion: triple helix technopolis

The triple helix model suggests that the interaction of institutional spheres will induce nonlinearity, crossover, and coevolution. This process can be seen in a university incubator facility that transcends its origins as a site for faculty spin-offs by taking in firms from outside the university, typically based on a business concept utilizing existing technology in a new way. As these firms start to collaborate with one another, often incentivized by a government program, each infuses the other and a new innovation dynamic is set in motion.

Coordination of organizations in the innovation space is useful in order to aggregate resources; it may also reduce duplication of initiatives and encourage creative expansion of missions. A science park that has been open to all firms may decide to focus on a particular theme to get involved in cluster-building. A research center may be created to infuse this cluster with advanced knowledge and technology. The technology transfer office and incubator facility may then interact with a cluster of firms that has the capabilities to utilize university resources.

Gaps may be creatively filled through initiatives based upon collaboration among innovation organizations. In embarking on such an effort, it is useful to analyze strengths and weaknesses across the landscape. This analysis may be done at the local, regional, national, or multinational levels and by institutional sphere. Once an initiative is undertaken to improve innovation, it must continuously be revised and adapted as technologies rise and fall and as innovation spaces expand and contract. The following chapter addresses the issue of the adaptation of the incubator, a prototypical innovation mechanism, to address a variety of opportunities.

7   The incubation of innovation

The incubator is an expression of the university's educational mission as well as its economic development and service missions. The incubator carries out the university's educational mission in a broader sense by expanding the traditional academic format of teaching individuals into one of teaching organizations. Although the incubator is traditionally defined as a support structure, providing common services to support firm-formation, incubation is fundamentally a method of training a group of individuals to work well together as an organization. The reconceptualization of the incubator as an educational institution takes the conventional notion of the incubator, adapted from the hospital machine to assist premature babies, a further step.

The university incubator is a relatively new concept, dating from the mid-1970s. A liaison official at the University of Colorado, Boulder, told the story of how he had received a phone call, some years ago, asking if the university had an incubator facility, and had referred the caller to the Poultry Science Department at Colorado State University. Today it is common knowledge, well beyond regional economic development circles, that the incubator paradigm has been extended from the hatchery and the hospital nursery to the academic and business worlds.

Beyond firm-formation, incubation is part of a broader framework for filling gaps in clusters, increasing the organizational density of regions and introducing new organizational capabilities into society. The incubator has been utilized to assist firm-formation from early-stage technology, to raise the technological level of existing firms, and to create jobs in distressed regions. Incubation has also been extended beyond the business firm to assist the development of cooperatives, arts groups, and non-governmental organizations. This chapter discusses the evolution of the incubator from a support mechanism for high-tech firms to a methodology for creating organizations to achieve a range of objectives.

Incubation of innovation

University incubators were originally established to speed up knowledge flow and technology transfer from university to industry. The normal academic process is to write a paper, present at a conference, and eventually publish in a journal. People in industry were expected to learn and adopt new ideas as an audience to this academic process or by hiring graduates. The slow pace and other limitations of this method led to several innovations to improve the transfer process, including the adaptation of the incubator concept from industry to assist academics with little or no business experience to start new firms based on technology invented in the university.

The format for incubation follows the normal academic educational process. There is typically an admissions procedure according to a set of guidelines similar to the criteria that universities follow in admitting individual students on the basis of past accomplishments and future promise. These include the qualifications of the firm's founders as well as the expected contribution of the firm to the economy and to society. Once the firm has been admitted to the incubator, the director may offer strategic advice and help it get more opportunities, much as an academic adviser helps students achieve their goals. Short courses may be available on specific topics such as marketing and business-plan development. Learning from informal interaction with firms at various stages of the incubation process also occurs, much as individual students learn from association with their peers. Finally, the stay in the incubator, typically limited to the approximate length of an undergraduate degree, may be concluded with a graduation ceremony.

University incubators originally focused upon realizing the commercial potential of academic research. This approach was revised when former employees of large companies asked if they could also locate their "close-to-the-market" start-ups in the incubator. These technology firms were often admitted on the basis of available space in the facility and their ability to pay the rent. Some entrepreneurs were simply interested in moving their firms out of their homes to a prestigious location; the common support services and easier access to university facilities, faculty, and students attracted others. The university incubator thus included a mix of academics and businesspeople starting firms in the same place, with each side learning from the other.

Origin and development of incubation

Incubators arose from a confluence of public and private interest in systematizing the transition from invention to innovation. The sources included inventors seeking to develop their ideas, corporations seeking to spin off technologies not directly related to their core competencies, universities seeking to transfer technology, and municipalities wanting to foster economic development. Based upon industry precursors, the initial objective was to assist the formation of firms from university research. During the early postwar period there were increasing numbers of university-based start-ups, especially near MIT and Stanford.

Renssellaer Polytechnic Institute (RPI), located in Troy, New York, a declining industrial region that was home to a great industrial research laboratory, wished to become involved in promoting start-ups. RPI realized that it needed a systematic method to foster firm-formation and imported the incubator concept from its neighbor in Schenectady, New York, the General Electric Corporation, for this purpose. Dr. Pier Abetti moved from the research lab of General Electric to assume a professorship at RPI, bringing the incubator concept with him.

Combining a strategy of academic and regional development, the contemporary university business incubator is part of a complex of organizational innovations targeted at the application of science to invention and of finance to the commercialization of research. These include the invention of the industrial research laboratory in the late 19th century, the technology transfer office in the early 20th century, and the venture capital firm in the early postwar period. University, government, and industry each undertake activities that move them away from classical arrangements into new hybridized formats such as entrepreneurial science, corporate university, business intelligence, and so on. The incubator, as a support structure to nurture the growth of technology firms, provides a location for some of these hybridized roles in the university.

The proto-incubator: Edison's "invention factory"

The origins of the incubator as an organizational entity can be traced to Thomas Alva Edison's efforts to systematize the invention and commercialization of technology. Edison's so-called "invention factory," founded in the late 19th century, widely recognized as the precursor of the industrial research laboratory, may also be seen as the prototype of the incubator facility. Edison created his systematic method for invention, long before the term "incubator" was applied to an organization designed to nurture the growth of high-technology firms, but his organization may appropriately be viewed in terms of the incubation process.[1]

Edison brought together technologists, scientists, and support staff in a single organization, to systematically design and patent a series of core technologies and develop spin-off firms to bring them to market. More than a support structure supplying research and technology to meet the needs of an existing firm, Edison's operation regularly and successfully created new businesses and industries such as film and sound recording, but also failed in developing cost-effective techniques to process low-grade iron ore.

The proto-incubator revolved around the technological vision of a single person who envisioned technological and business opportunities and then designed technical and organizational solutions to fill them, such as the electric light system. The General Electric Corporation, in various national formats, was founded to supply the needs of this new technological complex and advance its development through research efforts. It is perhaps not an accident that General Electric was one of the originators of corporate incubation in recent decades.

The early venture capital firm

The second source for the development of the incubator concept was the invention of the venture capital firm as a support structure for the early stages of firm-development. In contrast to the invention factory model based on the technical and business vision of a single individual, the original venture capital firm was designed as a selection mechanism to attract and winnow the technology ideas of a large number of persons. Although American Research and Development (ARD) sometimes used available space at MIT to locate firms, in essence it operated as a virtual incubator, attracting, selecting, and supporting ideas for new technology businesses.

The entrepreneurial incubator

The third source for the development of the incubator concept is an extension of the corporate R & D or development lab. Some projects that were considered "far out" or that had potential for the development of new business, or that were not directly related to the firm's existing activities, were removed from the lab. They were relocated to a separate space or unit where their champions could be given greater leeway outside the regular organizational chain of command. These undercover corporate R & D sites were sometimes called "skunk works." Originally the name for the home of an advanced aerospace project, companies such as Control Data and General Electric took the skunk works concept a step farther and established internal incubator facilities to encourage development of new technologies not necessarily related to the core business of the firm.

The corporate incubator serves as a test site for both employee and sponsoring firm. Corporate employees could retain their jobs while forming a new firm, returning to their previous job without great risk if the project did not work out. The company could encourage the low-cost development of new technologies by sharing with other investors the cost of spinning out firms, while retaining the right to purchase these firms at a later stage. However, when the corporation came under economic pressure, activities such as incubation that did not contribute directly to the bottom line were often closed down. Corporate incubation has been an episodic process that nevertheless continually reappears, especially when a firm finds that it needs to be more flexible or requires additional income from its R & D. Some large firms, for example Xerox, have recently made incubation into a recognized profit center.

The private incubator

In recent years, incubators have been established as independent firms or as spin-offs of venture capital firms. The private incubator, such as Idea-lab or Launchpad 39, is typically initiated by an entrepreneur, or group of entrepreneurs, and is tightly focused on a particular technology theme, such as the Internet, with the goal of developing a stable of closely related firms. The private incubator supplies capital as well as business and support services to entrepreneurs to grow their firms; it works off a common business model of firm-formation to guide its entrepreneurs.[2] The private incubator may even provide the business concept and, in effect, "hire an entrepreneur" to make it into a firm.

The private incubator represents a partial return both to Edison's original model and to the early venture capital firm. Since the incubator supplies capital, it takes equity on this basis as well as in return for assistance with firm development. The private incubator brings the incubator model full circle to Edison's concept of spinning off firms from a related set of technologies, and to the early venture firm model of providing extensive business and financial assistance. Private incubators have been called "networked incubators" since they tend to emphasize synergies among resident firms and even form firms for this purpose. In another sense a private incubator is an industrial district writ small, with firms interacting and doing business with each other at different levels of the supply chain, sharing information, cooperating as well as competing.

The state of the art

The incubator concept has spread across the academic world, within the US and internationally, following distinctive trajectories in response to varying academic, technological, and regional conditions.[3] There has been a focus on reverse-engineering and adapting imported technology in Eastern Europe, on spin-offs from faculty research in the US, and on student-organized firms in Sweden. Incubators have grown especially rapidly in China and Brazil. For example, in the early 1990s, Rio de Janeiro and New York City each had two university-based incubator facilities. Currently Rio has ten and New York three, although additional facilities are projected. One hypothesis to explain this difference is that New York's universities are highly competitive with one another, in contrast to Rio de Janeiro where the leading universities collaborate in assisting newer, smaller universities to develop their incubator facilities.

Similarities and differences among universities in different countries are reflected in different modes of incubation. In Italy, which is regarded as lagging behind in the development of new technology-based firms (NTBFs), incubators located in science parks have been found to play a significant role in remedying this deficit, with incubated firms demonstrating "superior post-entry performances than non-incubated ones, especially as regards growth rates."[4] According to the National Business Incubator Association, "Business incubators catalyze the process of starting and growing companies by providing entrepreneurs with the expertise, networks, and tools they need to make their ventures successful."[5] The concept has been realized at a wide range of technological levels and with different types of firms, as well as with non-firm entities such as NGOs and cooperatives and even with individual artists and craftspersons.

There are approximately 3,000 incubator facilities worldwide of varying scale and scope.[6] One of the fastest growing incubator movements is in China, where large-scale state-supported incubators typically grow several dozen high-tech firms simultaneously.[7] The incubator movement with perhaps the broadest scope is in Brazil, where several types of incubators have been invented to mentor low-technology firms, cooperatives, and NGOs, as well as high-tech firms. Although incubation occurs in a variety of settings to achieve a number of objectives, the basic elements of the incubator model include:

- a selection process, encouraging the improvement of the nascent business or organizational idea;
- subsidized space, available for a limited period of time;
- shared services, allowing support activities to be outsourced from the individual firm;
- mentoring and education in best practices; and
- networking, introduction to potential partners and investors.

To these basic components may be added the provision of a significant investment in the firm upon qualification for admission into the incubator. While many academics have unrealistic expectations for their inventions, the process of preparing a business plan for entry into an incubator can provide a reality test. Ideally, the firm-formation process clarifies business and technology concepts.

Stanford University does not have an incubator but it has been said of Stanford that the entire university is an incubator. A university with an entrepreneurial tradition located in an environment that has an informal support structure for firm-formation may not need an explicit facility devoted to that purpose. However, an organization designed to support firm-formation can help a university, especially one newly taking on an entrepreneurial role, achieve that goal. The premise of the incubator is that firm-formation can be improved by organizing it as an educational process, with formal and informal aspects. By bringing together various elements to improve firm-formation in a common setting, the goal is to increase the chances for success of new enterprises.

Contemporary incubator model

The contemporary university incubator revives the classic venture capital model, combining financing and mentoring of newly founded high-technology firms, originated by ARD in the early postwar period. The incubator adds value to the original venture capital model by locating various firm-formation activities, often along related technology themes, in a common physical space where cross-fertilization among companies can more easily take place. By reconnecting the incubator model to a venture capital process, new enterprises can systematically be created from various sources including, but not limited to, academic, industrial, and government research laboratories. Ideally, the incubator is part of a broader strategy of academic and regional co-development and a web of informal and formal university–industry ties. Such ties can be initiated through the creation of a formal structure, such as an incubator or a liaison office, or may arise from continuing relationships between professors and former students.

Firms may also be incubated from new business models created by entrepreneurs and academics and from incremental innovations developed within the non-research parts of existing firms. As a support structure for entrepreneurship, incubation is the logical next step after entrepreneurial education, even though historically it has typically come first, with an educational process added on later. Researchers' alertness to the economic implications of their research is the necessary condition for knowledge-based economic growth, while the existence of mechanisms to realize these implications is the sufficient condition. However, these possibilities are immanent and require nurturance, mentoring, and incubation to be realized; otherwise they remain merely potentials.

Incubation and the entrepreneurial university

As the academic entrepreneurial paradigm takes hold, interface capabilities spread throughout the university. Within academic departments and centers, faculty members and other technical personnel may be assigned special responsibility to assess the commercial salience of research findings and encourage interaction with external partners. For example, a faculty member in the Columbia University Medical School divides her time between traditional academic and technology transfer responsibilities. The incubation process can also have a positive effect back on research and teaching at the university. The incubator at the State University of New York at Albany enhances the research capabilities of the university by incubating new research centers and firms. Firms in the incubator collaborate with professors from the university and with laboratories from the state government. New research projects and new joint research centers have been organized through these collaborations.

There is no longer an assumption of a starting point of research and an end point of the economy or a single source of firm-formation. Incubator firms at various stages of technology push and market pull move further along the firm-formation trajectory from different starting points. The aggregation of a group of new enterprises from various sources at a single site also simplifies the search process for investors seeking projects. Investments can be made at the point of admission into the incubator, at the mid-point of their residence, and after graduation, in a three-tiered process. After additional review of the companies, funds can be invested in the best firms to assist their growth and movement out of the incubator.

Networked incubation

The incubator, traditionally considered an individual entity connected to a particular firm or university, may be reconceptualized as a broader model for "networked incubation." Networking was always part of the format of the incubator, seeking synergies among its firms, and an important task of the incubator director, seeking external resources to assist firms.

Networking can be enhanced by extending networked incubation from individual firms to incubators and from individual networked incubators to networks of incubators. It is useful to categorize incubators according to their networking dynamics:

- *intra-networking*, or operating through internal networks among firms within incubators;
- *inter-networking*, or operating through external networks among incubators and among firms from different incubators; and
- *extra-networking*, or operating through the formation of new organizations in incubators from heterogeneous entities.

In the case of the latter two types, it is also instructive to view these networking formats in relation to the research intensity of the particular academic institution and level of available resources in the region.

Private incubator: intra-networking

The private incubator typically starts from a single business idea, something of a departure from the classic university incubator, which theoretically is open to ideas for firms from all parts of the university. In the private incubator, the overall business concept is apportioned among constituent firms, which at a very early stage start doing business with each other. The firms are expected to complement, and give contracts to, one another. For example, in Internet businesses, a firm with expertise in graphics might provide that service to other firms.

Brazilian incubator movement: inter-networking

Since the introduction of the incubator concept in the mid-1980s, incubators have developed rapidly in Brazil, gaining support not only from universities, their original sponsors, but also from government at federal, state, and local levels and from industry associations. In federal and state universities with a strong "public" tradition, there was initially considerable resistance to incubators among many faculty members on the grounds that they represented the "privatization of the university." Instead of building new facilities immediately, early Brazilian incubators, such as the one at the Federal University of Rio de Janeiro, developed firms in temporary space, incubating themselves. When the director of the incubator, Mauricio Guedes, gained construction funds from the municipality, the issue of official university approval was brought to a head.

Resistance to the university mentoring private businesses did not halt the introduction of incubation but instead inspired a creative transformation of the incubator concept to fulfill the university's public mission in nontraditional ways. To create jobs, "people's cooperatives" were formed by the Graduate School of Engineering (COPPE) of the Federal University of Rio de Janeiro. The university invited low-income people from neighboring *favelas* for training, shaping them into a group cooperative to perform services and then sending them out into the world as an organization. The cooperative incubators were seen as successful and were extended through a national program to other parts of Brazil.

Other levels of government—state and local—also became involved. For example, municipalities took notice of the innovation and supported the growth of incubators by providing financing and other help. Incubators were started not only by universities but together with municipalities, and not only in the cities that had universities but in other municipalities as well. An incubator movement arose through these various sources of support. Several permutations of the university business incubator have been created, such as the "hotel for firms," a pre-incubation space for the firm-founder to hone their concept, find partners, and raise funds. The Brazilian national government, which from the 1970s had put most of its S & T resources into large projects, began to redirect its efforts, especially in an era of reduced funds, to assist incubator development.

Networking among incubators, and among firms from different Brazilian incubators, occurred extensively. For example, at the incubator in the Federal University of Fluminense (UFF) a firm developing educational software for schools was based on a software platform from a firm in another incubator. A network of experienced directors mentored the director, who had come to the job from the university library. The Rio de Janeiro network meets on a monthly basis to discuss common issues. The national meetings of ANPROTEC bring academic analysts of incubation together with incubator directors and personnel, providing an ongoing feedback of research to the incubation process, sponsored by the association itself, as well as by Brazilian research agencies. Networking helps explain the rapid growth of the incubator movement, especially to universities and municipalities with less than optimum resources.

Albany model: extra-networking

The extra-networked incubator, exemplified by the Albany model, brings together heterogeneous elements from various sources to create new hybrid organizations. The university at Albany lacked a sufficient research base to systematically develop new technology firms, the traditional incubator function. To generate critical mass, the incubator director invited local high-tech start-ups, R & D units of larger firms, laboratories of the state government, and research groups from the university into the incubator. The objective of locating these various groups together was to develop proposals to attract significant research funds from the state and federal governments. Individually, each entity would not be credible in making a large proposal; jointly they were. Thus the Albany incubator became an incubator of research centers.

Frederick Terman built Stanford into a research powerhouse after World War II by concentrating on "steeples of excellence," or selected areas of faculty expertise.[8] He held that it took a generation to achieve academic distinction in a field. Thus the emerging role of the Albany incubator was intended to be that of "research accelerator" to speed up the academic development process. A university official stated the problem, in a personal interview, as follows: "We don't have the resources of a major research university; we aspire to be a major research university so we are looking at non-traditional paths to get to that goal." Several centers were organized along the themes of the Albany incubators, one in biotechnology and a second in the areas of micro-electronics, semiconductors, computers, software, and atmospherics.

Organizational technology transfer

The incubator has primarily been seen as a stand-alone entity, yet networked in its region, a member of an association in its country or even linked through associations cross-nationally. But what about the firms in the incubator; how can they be linked globally? How can they be introduced to each other? The need for international linkage was expressed in visits to incubators such as Symbion in Copenhagen, where there were software firms interested in identifying customers for their products in

New York City multimedia firms. SOFTEC, a Brazilian government agency, has established offices in several US cities to play an introductory linking role for software start-ups and growth firms.[9] Such efforts, to date, are typically occasional and bilateral rather than systematic and multilateral, although SOFTEC points the way to a more systematic format.

New small technology-based firms typically face a problem of lack of market representation abroad. An incubator at the National Technological University in Norway has addressed this issue by stationing a representative at an incubator in Palo Alto. Nevertheless, this is a relatively unique solution which solves the problem only on a single point-to-point axis. Various mechanisms exist for transferring "hard" technologies; the transfer of "soft" organizational technologies is happenstance. Sometimes it occurs through professional tourism as visitors of various nationalities took the Stanford science park model or the RPI incubator model back to their own countries.

The state of the art of incubator firm interaction is characterized by individual bilateral cooperation informally supported by associations of incubators and their directors. Collaborations come about because someone knows someone else in a particular place and is able to establish that link through a personal relationship. Attending the US National Business Incubation Association (NBIA) or similar conferences can help establish that connection.[10] However, if an entrepreneur does not have the opportunity to attend incubator meetings in other countries, or does not have international ties through family or personal networks, the process requires some assistance.

A World Innovation Network

Incubators typically lack the ability to assist their firms to reach partners and markets in other countries. This is especially a problem in developing countries and small nations. A mechanism is required to systematically organize incubator networking across regions and countries. The concept for a World Innovation Network (WIN) is to do for incubator firms what an incubator does for its firms—provide a support structure to enable them to extend their activities into a broader arena and thereby enhance their chances of success. A small staff would coordinate and facilitate introductions and collaborations among its members. For example, an incubator firm in one country might need a partner to assist in developing its product or might wish to locate a sales representative at an incubator in another country. At present such arrangements typically happen by chance.

International technology transfer is primarily accomplished in three ways at present:

1   internally within the multinational corporation that has the ability to transfer a technology created in one of its units to others around the world;
2   as a negotiation between two discrete organizations from different countries, one a sender and the other a receiver of the technology, who may meet at a trade show or similar venue; and
3   via intermediaries, for example a university technology transfer office, like the one at Boston University that identified a market for an invention of one of its professors in a biotechnology firm that was a member of the Medicon Valley regional organization in Scandinavia.

There are also technology transfer firms, specialized for the purpose, but they primarily operate as listing services on the Internet, on behalf of universities, or as search services on behalf of large corporations.

What is missing from this picture is an organization that has the capabilities to collect and catalog information about the technologies available in incubator firms worldwide. Such an organization should also have the capability to take the initiative, to identify cooperation opportunities and potential partnerships, as well as to respond to requests for assistance from firms. The multinational corporation, the strong model of international business connections, provides a clue as to how to fill this gap. Presently, there are only informal and loose connections at the international level. However, if we look at the Brazilian networked incubator model, there is an emergent organizational linkage model already implicit in the incubator movement.[11]

A broader framework for international networking can be derived from the model of Brazilian incubators as members of networks, sharing projects among firms from different incubators. This model of networking incubators and incubator firms should be raised from the national to the international level. What is needed is a very small organization to operate an introduction or "dating service" taking the information about what is going on in firms in different incubators around the world, not in every firm and not in every incubator, but in those with firms that have technologies with international potential. Those are the ones to focus upon.

A more systematic way to network start-up firms, internationally, is needed. The incubator has traditionally been a support structure for the creation of firms; other mechanisms have been created and applied to linkage problems. For example, the technology transfer office is as a search mechanism, on the one hand, looking within the university for research with the potential to be commercialized and, on the other hand, looking for a market externally. An organizational capability, similar to that of a technology transfer office, should be introduced into the empty space between incubators to link their firms. It requires persons knowledgeable in both technology fields and incubator networks to make introductions.

Such pro-active and conversant staff members would then follow up to address issues in the emerging relationship. This process will build trust and cohesion in the incubator world.

Incubator cooperation can also be enhanced through social technologies such as video-conferencing and "dating-service" software, as well as through data-mining formats that can be creatively applied to this problem. There is a need to think in terms of upgrading the networking capacities and common services of incubators. Traditionally, phone-answering and fax machines were the common services offered. The Internet has moved us from thinking of the computer as a stand-alone entity. We now think of the Internet as a linking mechanism among computers and people. We should also be thinking of how to create new kinds of linking mechanisms for firms in different incubators. In the past, common incubator services meant shared capabilities within an individual incubator facility; the future selling point of common incubator services will be the ability to bridge different incubators internationally.

The future incubator will not be an individual entity but an integral part of networks of expertise and capitals, financial, social, and intellectual. Bringing together leadership of the various national incubator associations to exchange ideas is a worthy objective but the long-term goal should be to encourage firms from different incubators to collaborate on mutual projects such as marketing agreements, moving their products from one country to another. The long-term objective of the incubator movement is, after all, the creation of new firms with products that have an international reach. An organization is required to accomplish this networking agenda that represents both an innovation approach and business opportunity. The project could be supported by the national incubator associations as part of their international collaboration and they should ideally participate as stakeholders as well.

The incubator of incubators

Networking can also systematize the process of organizing incubators by formalizing the Brazilian model in which an older incubator facility at a large university serves as an informal hub, mentoring and benchmarking newer incubators at smaller universities. A model incubator or "incubator of incubators" may be established as the central node of a network of incubators and as a training facility for future incubator directors. This concept brings together the organizational training of students in Swedish entrepreneurship programs with the networking of incubators in Brazil into an entity explicitly designed as an educational facility to train incubator directors and firm-founders in firm-formation and networking.

The "incubator of incubators" concept for a model training facility and linkage node is especially useful to begin the incubation process in a region or country, such as Honduras, lacking incubators until quite recently. Such a facility could send out trained people from the "mother" or hub incubator to staff "daughter" incubators. For example, from an initial site in San Pedro Sula, incubators could be replicated in other cities and towns in Honduras as part of a network to promote technology transfer and diffusion of new business models. The Polytechnico Milan has recently adopted this model to link incubators at its satellite campuses in the Lombardy region to the main campus in Milan.

Principles of incubation

Incubation is also part of a general model for the management of knowledge and technology in regional development. Science-based economic development efforts typically utilize a series of organizational innovations such as science parks and research centers as well as the incubator. The principles of incubation are thus broader than the particular organizational format of the incubator and can be expressed in the following propositions:

- The development of science and technology is increasingly embedded in the triadic relationship of university, industry, and government.
- Institutions in each sector (academy, government, and industry) play hybridized roles that move them away from classical understandings of the sector, for instance entrepreneurial academics, academic industrialists, and business strategy in government.
- Incubators are organizations that internalize the triadic relationship and encourage and provide a home for these hybridized roles.
- Networking at various levels, among incubator firms, incubators, and institutional spheres, has the potential to enhance the rate of innovation and inventive activity, both technological and organizational.
- High-tech innovation is universalized as developing countries with the ability to develop human capital in niche areas are able to translate these competencies into internationally competitive technologies and firms.
- University entrepreneurship programs and incubator facilities have the potential to turn technology transfer from a linear north–south flow into an interactive process.

These elements are present to various degrees in any incubator program. The incubator is a flexible model that can be creatively adapted to the needs of countries and regions at different levels of technology and business development. Incubation may be formulated as a set of norms (a) and counter-norms (b):

1a A selection process for admission to the incubator encourages entrepreneurs to formulate their business ideas carefully for evaluation by committees of business and technical experts. The application and decision-making process by which new enterprises are accepted into the incubator is important in identifying firms with potential for growth and other relevant criteria of success.

1b   On the other hand, some incubators operate according to the principle that "the entrepreneur knows best." If the business concept sounds sensible, if space is available, and if they can afford to pay the rent, admission is granted.

2a   Firms are located in a common venue so that entrepreneurs can interact, learn from each other informally, and possibly establish collaborations.

2b   Virtual incubators may host meetings to encourage "learning" among firms, and clubs of graduated firms may be organized to continue this process once firms have left the incubator.

3a   An experienced entrepreneur as director can mentor the founders of new firms. Ideally, the director should be familiar with the business, financial, labor, and technical communities in a region and be able to link firm-founders with external resources.

3b   It is not unusual, however, for incubator directors to be drawn from the ranks of university staff, having to learn on the job and, if fortunate, being mentored by experienced incubator directors from other universities.

4a   Experts in business and technology may be available as staff members to assist entrepreneurs in developing their firm to be more successful than they could by themselves. Some incubators have such persons on the permanent staff, working intensively with firms.

4b   Other incubator facilities may bring experts in as consultants, on an occasional basis, to assist firms with specific projects.

Conclusion: from the teaching laboratory to the teaching incubator

The incubator has evolved into a multifaceted entity for entrepreneurial education and innovation, with a broader purpose than developing firms from academic research. This development is based on the following:

1   the embedding of an incubator in the research or teaching mission of the university, or both;

2   the dependence of an incubator solely upon its own university or on a network across academia, industry, and government, at various levels; and

3   the relative presence or absence of incubation support services, including public and private start-up financing, in the region.

Entrepreneurial education should be conceptualized more broadly, not just as training for the engineering or the business student to encourage them to work together in the future, but as something that is appropriate for every student in the university. This is a model of education that is beginning to appear in Brazil and it has the potential to spread much more broadly. Education based on the incubator model can be developed for various groups of students throughout the university. Gustavo Cadena, the director of the incubator at the National Autonomous University of Mexico (UNAM), developed the idea of using the incubator as a training facility, to bring together engineering and business students. Instead of the different streams of students being educated separately, they would also have some common courses on entrepreneurship in a classroom at the incubator. Furthermore, there was the opportunity to work in incubator firms so that they might think in the future of starting new firms themselves.

Incubator evaluation should take into account regional resources and the incubator's ability to utilize them. Whether it makes sense for an incubator to develop its own services largely depends upon whether these services are already available in the region. A region that is rich in requisites such as venture capital may not have to develop them in direct association with the incubator. On the other hand, a region that is lacking such tools may find it necessary to combine them with the incubator project. The university at Stony Brook developed a series of initiatives, such as visits by lawyers and accountants, to compensate for its "greenfield" site on the outer edge of suburbia. On the other hand, the university at Albany saw no need for such measures since relevant services were readily available in the Capitol region and it made more sense for the incubator director to network his firms than to internalize services.

The incubation process may be viewed as a matrix, with some slots more or less filled and various gaps left open in different countries and regions. Incubator firms in most countries typically face the problem of lack of access to seed venture capital on reasonable terms. FINEP, the Brazilian national development agency, has launched INNOVA, a program to create funds to fill this gap, while Israel provides a grant of funds upon admission to its MAGNET incubator program. In Denmark, there is a fund to invest in incubator firms. In any case, the most productive incubation format will comprise various elements. The university is also a natural incubator that sometimes plays an informal entrepreneurial role in the incubation of companies.

The future trajectory of the incubator as an innovation mechanism can be predicted, in part, by reviewing the development of the teaching laboratory and its movement from the periphery to the center of the university. The teaching laboratory was invented in the mid-19th century as a method to train students in doing research at the University of Giessen in Germany. Professor Justus Liebig organized the laboratory in a former army barracks, a shed at the outskirts of the university. Today, we would not think of having a university science building without classrooms and laboratory integrated in the same structure. However, the incubator is still often at the outskirts of the university. In future university buildings, an incubator will be integrated into each department and research center.

8   Reinventing venture capital

Introduction

Venture capital, in its original conception as an engine of regional renewal, is much more than a financial investment mechanism. Linking
the financial, academic, and public spheres, venture capital originated as
funds and other assistance for the early stages of firm-formation in exchange for a share of ownership or equity in the new firm. It was part of
a strategy for science-based regional economic development based upon
academic research capacities and a range of university–industry interactions at MIT. This strategy built upon and extended this base, creating
a new organization combining academic analytical and business development capabilities.

The original objective of venture capital was the creation of new jobs
and economic opportunities, not super-profits. The original venture capital firm American Research and Development (ARD), having relatively
small amounts of funds to invest, was well suited to dealing with start-
ups that require relatively small investments at the initial stages of their
development. As the industry grew, the venture firm outgrew its original
purpose due to its success in attracting funds. As their financial resources
increase, venture capital firms tend to focus on the later stages of firm-
formation and growth as well as merger and acquisition activities among
existing firms. Moreover, since venture capital firms typically believe that
they can function most effectively as a small group of partners and associ-
ates, the trend toward large investments in later-stage situations is accel-
erated. The number of investments cannot increase significantly since the
careful examination required before undertaking an investment remains
the same, whether it is a large or small amount of funds.

An early-stage investment gap opened up as venture capital became
similar to traditional financial institutions. As firm-formation once again
becomes the lead item on the innovation agenda, the problem of providing seed capital reappears, especially in periods of economic recession when it is scarcest. Venture capital needs to be reinvented to operate

in the downturn as well as the upturn of the business cycle and at the earliest as well as the later stages of firm-formation and growth.

Venture capital

Venture capital professionalizes the search and selection process through an evaluation of the proto-firms' technology, management, and market prospects. After investing, the venture firm further seeks to increase the firm's chances of success by providing advice and assistance. As opposed to a "holding company" that might seek to retain ownership in a group of companies, the venture capital model also presumes an exit strategy, a clear idea for sale of the investment, privately or publicly, within a reasonable time period. What constitutes a reasonable period may be at issue. A firm may be sold to a multinational for a quick but certain profit, where it may stagnate or even be suppressed in a change of business strategy, before it has the chance to achieve high growth independently.

New technologies, such as electricity in the late 19th century, electronics and computers in the mid-20th century, and nano-technology at present, open up a potential for innovation. The ability to focus capital on the process of innovation is often missing. The venture capital model introduced early-stage risky investing, with safeguards, to a broader constituency of universities, investment banks and pension funds, traditionally oriented to low-risk investing. Heretofore, only an extremely wealthy individual or family could provide some of the elements of the venture capital model but even the Whitney and Rockefeller families soon chose to operate through professional venture capital entities.

The specific objective of venture capital is to reduce risk and increase returns on investments in new technologies by compressing time frames for firm-formation. The broader objective is to foster the realization of a business concept through the establishment of a new organization that has the ability to focus on a particular project. A variety of initiatives are encouraged, with a relatively modest level of funding at the early stages, in order to determine which are worth selecting for greater support. Since capital is spread over a variety of projects, a higher level of risk can be justified in each investment than if a single project had to be chosen at the outset.

Venture capital increases the likelihood for success of risky ventures by restructuring the relation between risk and reward in high-risk investing. From the perspective of this high-growth/high-risk regime, modestly successful ventures are considered relative failures. Nevertheless, this judgment may be tempered by time. For example, Ionics, a firm developing water purification technology that was one of ARD's early investments in the late 1940s, was viewed by some contemporary observers as a so-called "living dead" that lacked growth potential. It was said that the firm was supported by the head of ARD for personal reasons. Nevertheless, over the course of a half century, Ionics became a major company, a member of the *Fortune* 500, until it was recently acquired by General Electric.

Private venture capital focuses on financial returns. Regional development has become a side effect of venture firms' comfort with having their investment objects close at hand for personal inspection. Rather than aggressively seeking early-stage technology investments by visiting campus laboratories, most firms expect to be approached by people seeking funds. Following the lead of a few highly successful firms has become a strategy for other firms. Private venture capital tends to focus on a very few "hot" fields at a time and tends to fund a larger number of follower firms than the area can reasonably sustain. Thus to attain funding, a prospective firm has to promise higher gains faster. This leads to increased spending to gain market share in the hope of driving out competitors. Such a strategy may place a firm at risk of its existence, or at least subject to sharp cuts, if it is not soon realized.

Dilemmas of "scale" and "scope" in private venture capital

Although venture capital views itself as acting at the cusp of innovation, the private venture industry is typically a second rather than a first mover. The personal computer and the Internet both had a significant prehistory before they drew the attention of the venture community. Biotechnology is a notable exception, drawing investments shortly after the first practical method of splicing genes was achieved. In any event, most venture capital investments go into technology areas once they are validated and tend to stay within the bounds of a few areas until the next breakthrough category is created. Nanotechnology is currently making the transition to an accepted category of investment.

The contemporary private venture capital firm occupies an extremely favorable position. It has access to a variety of capital sources such as pension funds, universities, and well-to-do individuals. Moreover, a virtually endless number of individuals with ideas for firms and firms at various stages of development seek its attention. Publicity about ARD's founding resulted in a large number of proposals submitted and entered into the firm's logbook, many more than could be seriously considered. Stratagems to meet a venture capitalist and give a quick explanation of a business plan are devised to overcome the reality that there are very many more firm-formation projects than venture capital firms can consider, much less fund. Indeed, it is estimated that only one of a thousand projects submitted actually leads to an investment.

The point at which private venture capital enters a technological trajectory is also an issue. Although new technology creates new needs and opportunities, these may not be immediately perceived, especially if an older related technology is already in place. Given the existence of the large-scale mainframe computer, ARD was not certain of the market for the new smaller-scale minicomputer. Therefore ARD, as their venture capital firm, advised Digital Equipment Corporation (DEC) to produce circuit boards as its initial product since the need for a new type of computer was not yet clear. Although the delay did not affect DEC's success, it is indicative of the conditional conservatism of venture capital.

The Internet bubble of the late 1990s brought to light additional problems in the functioning of a private venture capital industry where investments were often made in superfluous firms. Many Internet firms were based on imitative business concepts due to easy availability of capital. Their hope of gaining market share was through large expenditures on advertising and staff salaries. This strategy left firms vulnerable to decline when business conditions changed for the worse. A herd effect wastes money since not only the three best candidates are funded but the fourth and fifth, with many new firms' minor variations representing little or no technological advance. The venture model's dark side was highlighted when venture capitalists attempted exits in 18 months or less, eschewing longer-term investments.

Public venture capital firms

The private venture capital firm, operating under a favorable legal and tax structure, generates an impressive amount of capital but must deliver the highest possible return to meet the financial goals of its managers and institutional sponsors. These strictures limit its ability to act at the early seed stages or in the downturn of the business cycle. A variety of public venture entities has been created in recent years to solve lack of early-stage funding, as well as to extend the venture capital format to regions where it has not been available. Nevertheless, it is argued that a normative bias in favor of private venture capital is justified on the grounds that expert knowledge in selecting investment opportunities in the private sector is superior to expert knowledge resident in the public sector. Sometimes, this is more simply stated as the inability of government to pick winners.[1] However, a closer examination of the modus operandi of government technology agencies suggests that they may be less subject to some of the flaws of the private venture industry such as downstream drift and the herd effect.

Several US federal and state government programs provide funds for firm-formation, despite relative lack of awareness of the existence of public venture capital. At the federal level, distribution of public funds to early-stage and small firms typically obeys the format of a basic research grant, slightly modified to include commercialization potential. The federal government has also played a role in guaranteeing funds of venture capital entities, a measure that helped expand the industry in its early years.[2] State government programs usually operate closer to the private venture model, making an investment in exchange for a share in ownership. In countries where an extensive role of the state in industry is well accepted, there is little, if any, difference between public and private venture capital in so far as the stage in the firm-formation process when an investment may be made or the terms on which it is made. In other countries, where a significant, but less extensive, role for government is acceptable, public funding is seen as a transitional stage and disappears once a private venture capital industry is established. In still other countries, where a role for the state in industry is not well accepted, public venture capital is a veiled process.

The role of the state in society influences the nature of venture capital, irrespective of whether the source of funding is public or private. The role of government in the founding of the US venture capital industry was largely limited to changes in the rules to allow pension funds to invest a small proportion of their monies in a more risky way. However, once the industry showed signs of success, government encouraged the development of venture-capital-like entities by traditional banks. In "high-state" societies, where a strong role for government is legitimate, especially in relation to industry, public venture capital operates openly. If the role of the state is so strong as to preclude a separate industrial sphere, as in a centrally planned economy, the concept of venture capital as an independent organizational entity is superfluous. By contrast, in "low-state" societies, skeptical of government, public venture capital is often hidden behind other formats for government support, such as research grants, and may not be perceived as venture capital. Under "low-state" conditions, government ownership of firms in exchange for funds is not allowed and seed capital funding is carried out in other guises.

Public venture capital in "high-state" societies

In countries with traditions of strong industrial policy, such as Sweden, Israel, and Brazil, venture industries were fostered by direct government intervention. After failing to establish a venture industry through government-run venture funds, Israeli policymakers decided to combine public and private elements. There were two levels: a first-level government-established fund, Yozma, seeded subsidiary funds and attracted private coinvestors to a second level of so-called "drop-down" funds, making the actual venture investments. Government encouraged private capital to invest in the second level of venture capital entities by coinvesting funds to reduce the perception of risk. When the new funds were successful and private capital was confident enough to act on its own, government was able to withdraw from the industry. The Brazilian National Development Agency (FINEP) established a similar process, with the additional component of a competition to select firms to make presentations of their projects at "venture forums" in different parts of the country. These meetings include a preparatory training program to teach entrepreneurs such skills as writing a business plan and negotiating for investment.[3]

It is often assumed that an organizational mechanism can be transferred from one society to another, without taking culture into account. Some of the frustration felt by senders and receivers could be relieved by understanding that organizations and institutions of the same name may play different roles in various societies. For example, an Israeli venture capitalist presumed that his country's Yozma venture model could simply be transferred to Italy but his Italian colleagues believed that a more convoluted approach was required to make a version of the model fit into the Italian public finance system and not be rejected as a foreign antibody.[4] Nevertheless, additional elements are indicated, such as the incubator network under construction at Milan Polytechnic and its outreach campuses, as well as the encouragement of patenting inventions made at universities.[5] The venture format is part of a broader economic and social development strategy, comprising institutional, cultural, and organizational elements.

Given a tradition of government playing an active role in industrial development, public venture capital in Sweden is organized similarly to private venture capital, with a share in ownership taken in exchange for an investment. The venture capital model has also been extended to research through the establishment of a series of foundations to promote innovation. These new entities were begun by redirecting the "Wage-Earners' Fund," created by a tax intended to allow government to purchase stock and own the country's major corporations. The Strategic Foundation plays some of the role of the National Institute of Health (NIH) and NSF, supporting both the very early stages of commercialization and the collectivization of research in larger-scale research entities such as centers. Elements of the venture model have also been adapted by the Swedish Knowledge Competency Foundation, which utilizes a "due-diligence" approach to negotiate and monitor projects. Sweden also pioneered the role of foundations as quasi-public venture capital entities.

Public venture capital in a "low-state" society

Public venture capital is driven underground in the US, where it is considered to be illegitimate for the federal government to be involved in industrial development. There is a single notable exception to this rule, a CIA-sponsored venture capital organization that takes equity. InQtel's founding was justified by the necessity to establish a familiar format to help the agency gain access to technology from high-tech start-ups.[6] Public venture capital has had low visibility; indeed the concept often lacks legitimacy. In 1997 the New York Software Industry Association sponsored two sessions on venture funding at its annual meeting; the private venture capital session attracted more than 200 participants; the one on government programs just five persons. At the 2002 meeting the distribution between the sessions was more equal, a likely effect of the collapse of the stock market bubble.

US public venture capital comprises various government programs, at the federal, state, and local levels, which provide funds to entrepreneurs and innovative firms to help them realize economic gain from scientific and technological advance. The federal sponsors of public venture capital expect to realize returns for society, in the long term, through the "spillovers" and other benefits, such as tax returns, that may be generated. However, a newly proposed amendment to the NIH Appropriations Act requests the agency to consider a more direct return. State government S & T programs, on the other hand, operate closer to the private venture capital model, both in time frame and in the making of investment decisions, and have more direct responsibility for creating jobs. For example, the Connecticut Innovation Agency takes equity and expects a private venture firm to coinvest, while the State of Texas offers a program of grants to firms at various stages of development to support applied research and technology transfer.

Public and private venture capitals are complementary, with government playing the role of seeding the private venture capital industry with future investment opportunities. Public venture capital shifts the endless-frontier model of a self-propelling dynamic of scientific and technological advance to a more interventionist approach, following a basic research funding model where the idea is to support something that is new and risky by definition. The technological areas of interest to government are broader, and often at an earlier stage of development, than ones that private venture capital is willing to consider.[7] In private venture capital the focus has too often shifted to incremental innovation, a new wrinkle on a proven business idea, accompanied by an experienced management team. By contrast, public venture capital, following the grant model of basic research, is able to assume a higher level of business risk and thus has a greater potential to promote discontinuous innovation.

Government programs, such as ATP and SBIR, review proposals on both technology and business criteria.[8] They typically utilize internal government experts for the technology review and retired industry specialists for the business review. Indeed, public venture capital may be more heavily weighted to the technical side in reviews, which paradoxically allows it to take more business risk on early-stage long-term technologies than can a private firm focused on the financial side. Thus the prohibition against government making profits from assisting new firm-formation may make these programs more effective by encouraging greater risk-taking. Certainly, the SBIR and ATP programs accomplish the purpose intended by the founders of ARD in the early postwar period, the initiation of a high-tech firm-formation dynamic from academic research.[9]

When the private venture capital industry is strong, technology entrepreneurs focus virtually all of their fund-raising attention on this source even though the success rate is much less than 1 percent. The success rate for gaining public venture capital in the US is approximately 15 percent. Half of US private venture capital was projected to disappear in the wake of the failure of Internet firms, in which much of it was heavily invested.[10] Even with such a precipitous decline the industry will still be larger than it was in 1996. In any event, public venture capital will continue to grow at the federal level as a function of public research funding. While private venture capital recedes, with downturns in the business cycle, federal public venture capital is stable since federal government appropriations are relatively impervious to economic downturns or, following Keynes, may even increase in the wake of recession or depression. State venture capital is subject to the business cycle since US states are required to maintain balanced budgets, even in the downturn.

Venture formats have also been invented to supply capital to support business concepts that do not meet contemporary venture capital requirements for investment to be considered of potential to achieve extraordinary profits. Business opportunities that fill important social needs in a community also require venture funding, even though they may make only modest profits. Utilizing the venture capital model of spreading risk among a variety of investments to meet social needs marks a return to the original purpose of supporting regional economic and social development that the venture industry was created to achieve.

A typology of venture capital

Various organizations and individuals have become involved in venture capital in recent years, making it available in fields that the private venture capital sector had departed, such as the very early stage, or where it had never existed, for example, in poorer regions. Operating from different criteria, and with various objectives, they have filled gaps and created new venture capital niches. As the early-stage venture capital gap is filled by the very organizations that produce the technology that becomes the basis for new firms, so universities, corporations, and public research institutes become venture capitalists. Venture capital was invented, in part, to play an intermediary role between universities, industry, and government. As the boundaries between the institutional spheres decline, the need for formal intermediary organizations may decrease. At the very least, organizations that previously relied on intermediaries believe that they can undertake some of these tasks themselves in subsidiary units.

University venture capital

A growing number of universities are forming venture capital arms, seeking a balance between transferring technological innovations produced within the university to existing firms, on the one hand, and spinning them out, on the other. These new firms are often led or assisted by faculty members and students, some of whom may become full-time members of the firm.[11] The organization that originates the technology thus has a better opportunity to participate in the value that is created. If technology transfer or venture capital is undertaken by intermediary organizations, the value created is less likely to return to the original source. Thus technology transfer has become an internal academic function during the past two decades; venture capital is following the same route.

Although Boston and Columbia universities have attempted to provide virtually the entire funding for new ventures, in biotechnology and distance learning respectively, most universities have pursued a more conservative strategy of spreading risk among a variety of ventures. Like Baylor University Medical School they provide seed funding at the early stage where private venture capital is often lacking and seek public and private venture capital for the follow-on stages. Baylor also identifies an entrepreneur to work with the academics who have originated the technology.

University venture capital returns to the early venture capital firm model, pioneered by ARD, of taking the lead in organizing a start-up company. In the very earliest stages of firm-formation, the firm and its leadership are an extension of the university's venture capital arm, rather than an independent organization, whatever its formal legal status. University and corporate venture capital follow a similar format in hatching new companies within their organization. The advantage for the nascent firm is access to the various facilities and resources of the parent organization, such as meeting rooms, equipment, etc. if a formal incubator facility does not exist.

Universities balance between earning royalty income in the short term from a technology licensed to an existing firm and achieving in the long term greater earnings through equity participation in a new firm, between contributing to regional economic development and earning maximum returns to support academic activities. Universities have the ability to take a longer-term perspective and are thus well suited to early-stage venture capital once they have developed a professional competence that has a relatively independent identity. The downside of university venture capital is the tendency to overcommit to a pet project of a faculty member or senior administrator rather than to pursue a professionally managed portfolio of early-stage investments. Of course, firms initiated by university venture capital arms, which require large follow-on investments, may be carried forward in partnership with other sources of private or public venture capital.

Corporate venture capital

Corporations and universities moved into the field as venture capital firms became successful, aware that they were the source of much of that success. Although firms and academic institutions contain the nuclei of new firms that could be spun out, they are often conflicted about how to support firm-formation. Firms are concerned about maintaining current "core competence" versus renewing that competence to insure future viability. Corporate venture capital seeks to capitalize knowledge that is not directly relevant to a firm's core competency. It also seeks to modernize the firm by creating business units that may be the basis for the transformation of that competency. Corporate venture capital functions best when it works close to areas in which the corporation has competence but is also subject to the financial strictures of downturns when companies tend to reduce nonessential activities.

Can a large corporation, which by definition has an established range of products and technologies, become a successful venture capitalist, either within its traditional business area or outside of it? The evidence is mixed but tends toward the negative. Firms have to balance between commitment to their existing businesses and the desire to establish new business activities within and without the firm. Even if the goal is to utilize quasi-venture mechanisms to establish new business units within the firm, there is a possible tension between growing these units through internal technology transfer from R & D laboratories to existing business units, on the one hand, and establishing new divisions, on the other. The inability to resolve some of these tensions explains why some internal corporate venture capital activities are closed despite apparent financial success.[12]

Three waves of corporate venturing have been identified in the US from the 1960s. In each wave, after initial enthusiasm most firms exited the industry.[13] For example, after investing in 19 internally generated ventures from 1970 to 1981, Exxon left the field after finding that none had achieved commercial viability. Kodak had a similar experience during the 1980s during the so-called second wave of corporate venturing. Xerox had difficulty envisioning how to make successful businesses out of new technologies, such as the "mouse" and the laser printer, that it had successfully generated at its laboratory in Silicon Valley. Apple Computer, a new firm supported by private venture capital, soon learned about these products and took them to market. The contradictory nature of corporate venture capital, and the difficulty of deciding whether spin-off or spin-on (creating an independent firm or using the technology internally) is the objective, increase the uncertainty of corporate venture units within the sponsoring firm and may explain their periodic closure and reinstatement.

Corporate culture significantly influences the success or failure of venturing projects. For example, 3M has had considerable success in encouraging employees to develop new business ideas within quasi-independent units. The firm is known for encouraging employees to develop new product ideas and for supporting that development. Developing new technologies in emerging fields is a specialized competence that needs to be embodied in units whose autonomy is protected. The periodic re-entry of large corporations into the venture field indicates that it is a potentially significant element of corporate renewal, like the central R & D laboratory. Of course, the venture capital process can be outsourced, with start-ups acquired as necessary from the venture industry. Since it can be very expensive to acquire an existing firm, there is a continuing incentive for large corporations to create a quasi-start-up process.

Foundation venture capital

Foundation venture capital is at a very early stage and relatively little is known about its operation. The Markle Foundation in the US, taking as its mission the infusion of technology into primary and secondary education, has made several investments in educational-software firms that could not meet the criteria of the private venture industry for market share and returns. The Knowledge Competency Foundation (KK) in Sweden has taken similar steps.

Foundation venture capital can activate private venture capital, providing a balance wheel for the industry in the downturn as well as a benchmark in the upturn. Thus Industrifonden, the publicly funded Swedish venture capital firm, established as a foundation that is independent of government control, solves several venture capital problems. For example, Industrifonden's strategy of spinning off semi-independent regional funds suggests a way to maintain focus on early-stage investment even as the scale of capital under management grows. Industrifonden has also helped private venture capital firms make follow-on investments that they might not otherwise have had the resources or courage to undertake, by partnering with them during the downturn.

There is a tendency for venture capital firms, as their capital increases, to become less involved in investing in the early stages of firm-formation. One obvious cure for this scale dilemma is to divide a larger fund into smaller sub-funds, with independent freedom to invest. Industrifonden, consisting of eight regional sub-funds, is located between the public and private spheres, making it impervious both to short-term market pressures and government intervention to withdraw funds. The director said,

> we have no owner . . . we are living our own life . . . during these 20 years, especially in '96, the legislation around the Foundation was strengthened. We are very much protected from different ambitions. We are living a very good life. We are making money, and we are not allowed to pay taxes.[14]

Sweden's Industrifonden is a successful experiment in public venture capital that should be examined for its potential to be replicated elsewhere.

Foundation venture capital serves as a benchmark and as a source of additional resources for the private venture capital industry in Sweden, which grew greatly in the 1990s but is currently in a period of restructuring. Several private venture firms have closed and the others are deciding which investment in their portfolio to keep alive, sometimes through co-investments with Industrifonden. The director of Industrifonden said that most staff members have a technical background and are typically "engineers with an academic background; 50 years plus; former presidents or other people from high positions [in companies]." The organizations' cadre of senior staff invests in early-stage technology firms at the rate of one per week.

Community development venture capital

Private venture capital, with its focus on high-growth fields and extraordinary profits, has been primarily associated with areas that have significant knowledge or financial strengths, rather than with rural or low-tech regions. Nevertheless, the need is felt for capital to support firm-formation in low-growth and slow-growth industries, in poor rural and urban areas, and in Native American communities that lack many of the prerequisites for the capitalization of knowledge such as an entrepreneurial university or a cluster of public research institutes. A community development-oriented venture industry has been established that funds food distribution and other sorely lacking enterprises in depressed regions, with joint public–private support, including the Community Development Financial Institutions Fund (CDFI) of the US Department of the Treasury.[15]

US Community Development venture capital, with 535 million dollars under management in 2002, includes 64 active funds, with 15 in formation, that pursue exit strategies but are not under pressure to produce high returns. Financial and social goals are balanced in making the investment decision. The objective is to develop a regional infrastructure, to create jobs and opportunities at a variety of levels of technology and business sophistication.

Angel investors and syndicates

Individual angel investors and angel syndicates have filled some of the "early-stage" gap opened up by the venture capital transition to later-stage investments. Individuals who have themselves been successful entrepreneurs often take this role as an alternative to retirement. Being "in the game" is often as important to them as the prospect of financial return, although, of course, that is always part of the equation. Such individuals are typically more willing to invest at the earliest stages and assume a greater risk. Whereas the venture capital firms are driven downstream by their increasing resources, angels tend to stay upstream where the smaller amount of funds that they typically have available can make a difference.

Angels may also become paid or unpaid consultants to firms, utilizing their business and technical expertise, as well as their funds, to assist the new venture. There are more potential angels than venture capital firms and thus the likelihood of an angel investment is higher. However, the greater publicity that venture capital firms have received means that entrepreneurs tend to chase after such firms even though their chances of receiving an investment are small or almost nonexistent. Indeed, it has been noted that many entrepreneurs are not even aware of the independent angel possibility, as a step beyond family and friends.[16]

The venture capital cycle

Private venture capital basically follows the business cycle. Funds expand in good times and even faster as the growth of a bubble accelerates. Venture investments in firms slightly lag behind the upturn of the cycle but then accelerate as "irrational exuberance" takes hold. A frenzied search for investment opportunities overcomes the conservatism of the venture capital "due-diligence" process in which potential investments are carefully researched before funds are committed. When the economy slows in recession or the bubble bursts abruptly the rate of venture capital investing slows or even comes to an abrupt halt. In regions lacking a tradition of firm-formation, potential investors often view investing in a new firm as too risky even in the upturn of the business cycle. Introducing public venture instruments can counter this negative attitude, reduce risk and break the barrier to firm-formation.

The venture capital cycle may be conceptualized as follows (SSBGG):

1 *Stasis*. Potential investors are fearful to commit funds to a new venture and therefore request such a high proportion of the equity of the firm that entrepreneurs are unwilling to accept a deal.
2 *Shortfall*. A nascent venture industry is established but venture firms are undercapitalized and, while they are able to make initial investments, lack sufficient funds to support follow-on rounds.
3 *Balance*. A venture industry is expanded with firms having sufficient funds to make a range of initial and follow-on investments at acceptable terms to entrepreneurs.
4 *Gluttony*. The amount of funds available to private venture capital firms increases rapidly, leading firms to move to the later stages of investing in firm-formation.
5 *Gap*. The shortage of venture funds for investment in the very early stages of firm-formation requires the reinvention of venture capital instruments to meet that need.

The US has gone through three venture capital cycles since the founding of the industry in the early postwar period while Sweden, a country relatively new to venture capital, has seen at least two cycles.

Countercyclical venture capital

A countercyclical model of venture capital is needed to remedy the dilemma of a private venture capital industry subject to the vicissitudes of the business cycle. Taken together, private, public, university, corporate, community, and foundation venture capitals have the potential to create an industry that is active in all phases of the business cycle and at all stages of the firm-formation trajectory. This mix of funds fulfills the original venture capital vision of creating economic growth from start-ups based on academic research and new business models, supported by the public sphere. An array of venture capitals, drawing upon diverse institutional resources across the triple helix, is required to make the transition from creative destruction, with significant gaps between techno-economic paradigms, to an endless transition of creative reconstruction, with new industries appearing before old ones disappear.

Venture capital instruments based on different institutional spheres have the potential to create an industry that can operate at all stages of firm-formation and in the various phases of the business cycle. For example, government and academia are capable of supporting longer time frames than industry and are therefore less subject to the vicissitudes of the business cycle. As we have suggested, the downturn is a propitious time to encourage start-ups since human capital is more available, with people leaving failed ventures or being laid off from survivors. Entrepreneurs are active and space is more available. Nevertheless, there is typically a lack of capital invested in start-ups; although funds are available, holders of capital are typically afraid to invest. The downturn should be the time at which the Schumpeterian ideas come fully into play; creative destruction is under way but creative reconstruction is elusive.

Countercyclical venture capital consists of an array of venture capital entities that are an expression of the strands of the triple helix as well as hybrids among them, including such public–private entities as foundations. Collaborations among organizations with a long-term perspective increase the solidity of their commitment to early-stage investing as well as the amount of funds available. For example, university–bank venture coalitions have been initiated in Belgium to support firm-formation from academic research.[17] The potential of private and government-funded foundations as venture capital instruments should be further developed to complement the private venture industry, providing a funding source for less-favored fields and less venture capital-intensive regions.

Conclusion: reinventing venture capital

Each type of venture capital corrects another's deficiency. Thus public venture capital focuses on the creation of new industries and jobs, seeking long-term economic growth. Public venture capital can maintain focus on early-stage investments, especially in societies where government is restrained from acting too close to the market. Government appropriations may be stable and should theoretically increase during a recession, when human capital and other resources for firm-formation are more available, but public money may be withdrawn as tax revenues decrease. University venture capital can take a long-term perspective and is able to operate at the early seed stage but may be diverted to support projects of influential faculty members. Foundation venture capital, with resources guaranteed by an independent legal structure, not subject to other organizational priorities, is the purest public venture capital instrument, able to focus on the early stage and act in the downturn. Foundation venture capital sets goals and distributes funds relatively autonomously but the establishment or redirection of foundations for this purpose is relatively limited, to date.

The chicken/egg dilemma of whether an entrepreneurial culture or the availability of venture capital is the most essential ingredient for firm-formation is unresolved. Nevertheless, an embryonic entrepreneurial infrastructure and the availability of a variety of venture capital formats is helpful to making the venture capital model work. Georges Doriot, ARD's founding director, tried and failed to transfer the venture model to his native France in the 1960s. Europe was not receptive to a start-up culture at the time but by the late 1990s the emphasis on government-sponsored "grand projects" abated and the cultural infrastructure in which venture capital could thrive began to appear. In the US, ARD, having originated at the mid-point of a public–private continuum, had long since been reconstituted as a partnership. By the late 1980s, ARD was one of perhaps a dozen venture firms still focused on early-stage technology investments.

The venture capital firm originated from a triple helix of university–industry–government interactions, but these helices drew apart with the growth of the venture capital industry. Private venture capital lost its social goals as the industry became a pure financial instrument. Nevertheless, some of the original purpose of venture capital as a method of regional development has been recovered through the creation of public and other alternative forms of venture capital. Having originated as an economic development strategy for a depressed region, venture capital has primarily been associated with emerging high-growth regions.[18] Nevertheless, venture capital has been applied to declining industrial and rural regions in formats that balance financial and social goals. Indeed, the venture capital firm was invented to achieve this very purpose.

9   The endless transition

Introduction

We have passed from an era based on an assumption that research automatically translates into use, to an era where policies are continuously reinvented to achieve that objective. Transcending the development of new formats for the production and distribution of knowledge, the endless-frontier idea of "priming-the-pump' organizational models for innovation is continually reinvented, reconceptualizing what a region does, what a firm does, what a university does, and what government does, individually and collaboratively.

The triple helix of innovation is emerging in widely different societies, with previous traditions of strong and weak levels of state activity. Government is taking either a more or a less active role in knowledge-based economic development. In countries that followed a linear model, there has been a shift to an assisted linear model, with intermediate mechanisms introduced to move research into use. An indirect and decentralized innovation policy, across the institutional spheres, may be more effective than traditional direct approaches since it is better able to take regional differences into account and incorporate bottom-up initiatives. Nevertheless, the goal is the same: how to build upon existing resources to create niches of technological innovation and secure a place within the division of labor in the global economy.

Beyond the "endless frontier" lies a continuous series of experiments on the relationship between science, industry, and government in creating the conditions for future innovation. The notion of transition was set forth in Eastern Europe after the collapse of Communism and one question was often posed: what is the endpoint of transition? The answer is that there is no endpoint: innovation is an endless transition. Nor are only the former Soviet Union and Central and Eastern European countries in transition; so too are the US, Asia, Western Europe, Africa, and Latin America.

Breaking boundaries—building bridges

The enhanced importance of science and technology to economic development is recognized in north and south, east and west. In some countries, there is a movement away from an assumption that there is a single starting point of research and an end point of the economy: a linear model in which things happen by themselves. It is also realized that it is necessary to start from the standpoint of problems in society, the reverse linear model, and to see how knowledge can be used to address them. It is increasingly the case that industrial firms need the application of knowledge to improve their production processes or to develop new firms on the basis of knowledge. It cannot be expected that entrepreneurs can do this by themselves.

In countries that, to one degree or another, relied on central planning, it has become accepted that government programs have an important role to play, not only from the national level—top-down—but also from the local level—bottom-up, often in collaboration with other organizations in civil society. When bottom-up initiatives that have proved successful, such as the incubator movement in Brazil, are reinforced by top-down policies and programs, perhaps the most dynamic and fruitful result is achieved. It also means that universities and other knowledge-producing institutions play a new role in society, not only in training students and conducting research but also in making efforts to see that knowledge is put to use.

The result is an interactive model, with intermediate mechanisms, that integrate the two traditional starting points of science-and-technology policy. In contrast to biological evolution, which arises from mutations and natural selection, social evolution occurs through "institution-formation" and conscious intervention. The triple helix provides a flexible framework to guide our efforts, from different starting points, to achieve the common goal of knowledge-based economic and social development.

Beyond the endless frontier

Land may end when an ocean is reached but science is an "endless frontier." While science is the ultimate source of much technology, research does not produce innovation by itself. As we have seen, incubators, science parks, and technology transfer offices harvest the economic potential of research and link science to the economy. The linear model has been revised and expanded into an assisted linear model, recognizing the creation of hybrid organizations through triple helix interactions as the method to produce concrete results from public R & D spending. Although the assumption of a direct hand-off of knowledge from university to industry has had to be abandoned, the linear model has not disappeared.

The linear model, often declared "dead" in the innovation literature, is like the mythical hydra who grows two heads when one is cut off. This persistent model of science-based innovation derives from one part of Vannevar Bush's endless-frontier report of the early postwar period,[1] providing justification for government support of research of various kinds to meet military, housing, health, and other social needs, as well as unfettered basic research with the expectation of eventual useful outcomes. The much-cited, but largely unread, report was transmuted into support for "no-strings-attached" basic research funding, which was only one aspect of Bush's synoptic program that included support for research primarily as a means of solving specific societal problems in housing, health, and transportation, as well as meeting military needs.

During the Cold War US science policy was based on dual premises, one overt and one implicit, relating, on the one hand, to the long-term utility of basic research and, on the other, to expected military applications. The end of the Cold War has brought with it a lessening in the force of military justifications. At the same time, international competition for US industry has led to pressures in the economy for shorter-term applications of research. A variety of measures have been put in place to achieve this goal, including an enhanced role for academic research and government-supported technology programs to spur industrial innovation.

Different technological areas had been thought of as being connected to different disciplines and different industries but they are now cross-fertilizing each other. Previously there were strong boundaries between individual disciplines. Moreover, as we have seen, new interdisciplinary synthetic fields with industrial significance have been created, such as bioinformatics, whose components came out of the previous syntheses that created computer science and molecular biology. Now these two have themselves been brought together to form a new field in a continuing process of combination and recombination that has created other new fields such as behavioral economics and nanotechnology.

The future legitimation of science

The contribution of scientific specialties, such as solid-state physics and molecular biology, to the growth of old industries and the foundation of new ones has given rise to a new ground for legitimation of science as the source of high technology. This theme harks back as well to the founding charter of modern science as set forth by Francis Bacon, in which science-based industrial growth and understanding of nature were joint and complementary purposes of science. This vision held sway until the late 19th-century split between pure and applied science, engineered by physicists such as Henry Rowland who believed they could generate sufficient support for their science. This cultural divide is currently disappearing under pressure from scarcity of resources and convergence between addressing areas of fundamental science such as the human genome and meeting societal concerns such as economic growth.

The increased relevance of science to future economic development means that funds for research must now be distributed to all areas of the country. It is no longer acceptable for funds to be distributed almost entirely to the existing centers of research that are concentrated in a few regions, primarily on the East and West Coasts and in a few locations in the Midwest. All regions want a share of research funding because they are now aware that it is the basis of future economic growth. That is why the peer system breaks down. That is why funding is made on other bases such as direct Congressional appropriations for research centers at local universities. These practical political considerations have been raised to an explicit policy level in Europe, where goals of achieving cohesion and rectifying regional imbalances are built into the European Union's framework programs for technological and economic development.

The traditional legitimations of support for science still hold: the cultural justification of science as an end in itself, and defense research. Health, of course, remains a strong stimulus to research funding. The future legitimation of scientific research that will keep funding at a high level is that it is the basis of economic growth.

The capitalization of knowledge

The idea that culture, including science, could be transformed into capital became apparent when it was seen to generate a stream of income. While some scientists, like Pasteur, expected their ideas to have industrial applications even though they were not personally interested in capturing financial rewards, it came as a surprise to others to find that their ideas had become the basis of entire industries. For example, sociologist Robert K. Merton, who invented the "focus-group" interviewing technique during the 1940s, was astonished to learn, years later, that a research method that he had played a part in developing during World War II to evaluate information campaigns to troops had become the basis of a multi-million-dollar advertising and political industry during the postwar period.

New dynamics of knowledge production

Rather than financial capital invading and controlling knowledge, the capitalization of knowledge arises from dynamics within knowledge production itself. The capitalization of knowledge denotes the transformation of knowledge into capital and the processes through which this takes place, such as intellectual property rights and the patent system, corporate research labs and consortia, technology transfer and liaison, venture capital (private and public), incubators, etc. As the capitalization of knowledge occurs, capital also gains more knowledge capabilities. This "cogitization of capital" occurs, as new methods are invented to appraise risk such as the Black/Scholes options-pricing algorithm. New types of organizations to assess risk, such as hedge funds and venture capital firms, search out and discriminate among potential candidates for investment.

The capitalization of knowledge has replaced disinterestedness as a norm of science. This new norm has arisen from the practices of industrial science and the emergence of an entrepreneurial dynamic within the university. It has also emanated from changes in the rules for disposition of intellectual property arising from government-funded research, and from direct industrial policies as well. The norm of capitalization has been embedded in organizations such as technology transfer offices and in the requirements of government granting programs to show broader impacts from research. The cogitization of capital is displacing "rule of thumb" and other tacit methods of investment decision-making. The methods and principles of organizing and producing knowledge have also changed.

Synthesis of hybrid disciplines

New disciplines are created through synthesis of various elements in contrast to the splitting off of new disciplines from old ones in the way psychology developed out of philosophy in the 19th century.[2] Syntheses of practical and theoretical interests, elements of older disciplines such as electrical engineering, a bit of psychology and philosophy, and a machine were made into computer science. Similar processes, combining government, industrial, and academic interests, were at work in creating material science and the other sciences that are on everyone's critical technology list.

A reciprocal relationship between practical and theoretical interests has led to a further series of new disciplines at the intersections between earlier syntheses. Synthetic disciplines with industrial significance, such as bio-informatics, are created whose components came out of the previous syntheses that made computer science and molecular biology. Now these two have themselves been brought together to form a new field in a continuing process of combination and recombination that has created such fields as behavioral economics and nanotechnology. A new department at the University of Washington was constituted through collaboration among academic disciplines, supported by the Microsoft Corporation as a window on an emerging area of knowledge with business potential. Syntheses among knowledge areas, organizational formats, and institutional spheres are the basis of a new model of innovation.

Mode 2?

An intriguing hypothesis has been set forth that science is currently undergoing a radical epistemological transformation: from research based on questions that arise within separate disciplines (mode 1) to an alternative format with researchers from different disciplines collaborating on projects that are sourced in practical issues (mode 2).[3] Parodoxically, the so-called mode 2 interdisciplinary research, with both theoretical and practical implications, is the original format of science from its institutionalization in the 17th century. So why did mode 1 disciplinary research, isolated from the context of application, arise after mode 2, based upon collaborations, networks, and invisible colleges?

A conceptual framework to explain the benefits to society of maintaining the ability of scientists to pursue their ideas, wherever they led, was needed to establish a sovereign space for science. Whereas mode 2 represents the material base of science, how it actually operates, mode 1 is an ideology constructed upon that base in order to justify scientific autonomy. Such concepts were especially important in an era when science was still a very fragile institution, and needed help to maintain its independence, as appeared to be the case in the US during the late 19th century. When holders of great industrial fortunes donated funds to found new universities, many observers felt that the industrialists making these gifts would try to shape these universities' directions. It was feared that these donors would influence the hiring and firing of professors as well as what topics were acceptable to be studied.[4]

The rise of the ivory tower

Concern about such possibilities was heightened by several cases in which academic freedom was breached by the firing of professors who had taken unpopular positions.[5] Professor Henry Rowland of Johns Hopkins University, as president of the American Association for the Advancement of Science, posited a sphere of science that would be beyond the control of economic interests. If external interests intervened in the university, it would harm the conduct of science. Therefore it was best that even philanthropists keep hands off. When universities were a weak institutional sphere, an ivory tower model, emphasizing isolation and de-emphasizing practical concerns, served to protect academic freedom.

The autonomy of science was strengthened by Robert K. Merton's theory of the normative structure of science.[6] This sociological theory of science as a self-organized and self-regulating social process defended the free space of science against attack by Nazi proponents of racialist ideas as science and from Lysenko's attempt to control biology in the former Soviet Union. The third element in establishing the independence of science was the 1945 report *Science: The Endless Frontier*.[7] The supply of practical results from science during World War II would have constituted a de facto justification. But with the end of the war and without awareness in advance of the effect of the Cold War and *Sputnik*, a rationale was needed in 1944 and Vannevar Bush, the head of the wartime Office for

Scientific Research and Development (OSRD), persuaded President Roosevelt to write a letter commissioning the report.

The World War II seamless web

During World War II the OSRD spent significant sums at universities to support advanced weapons development, often on projects proposed by academics. In the wartime programs, university researchers were linked to engineers from manufacturing companies. They often worked in each other's premises within the framework of government programs. The objective was to insure a seamless web from laboratory research to military equipment, with feedback from field experience. Government negotiated R & D contracts with universities that accepted their argument that part of the funds should support the infrastructural costs of the university undertaking the project.

The military research agencies established just after the war retained much of the integrated wartime model. This was the case in the Office of Naval Research (ONR) and then in the Advanced Research Projects Agency (ARPA), established after the 1957 lofting of the *Sputnik* satellite gave rise to fears that US science was falling behind that of its Cold War competitor. Program officers in these agencies were proactive, bringing together interested scientists from various universities and firms to work on projects that they often took the lead in initiating. DARPA, however, was an exception to the premise that government funding of research would lead to innovation by itself.

During the postwar era government funding of R & D came to be accepted as the basis of university research in complete contrast to prewar rejection of this same funding. The difference can be explained by two factors: scientists' realization of the efficacy of government funding in speeding the research process and their finding that they could achieve a relatively hands-off relationship with government, with significant funds distributed without direct control.

Assisted linearity

By the industrial restructuring of the 1970s it was apparent that transfer of knowledge from university to industry through publication and hiring of graduates was too slow in an era of intense international competitiveness. An unintended consequence of ideological opposition to direct government relations with industry led the US to adopt an innovation policy based upon "action at a distance." Given the resistance to an enhanced role for the federal government, when intervention is decided upon it is typically carried out indirectly.

Initiatives such as the Small Business Innovation Research Program extended the forward linear model downstream, following the general format of a basic research grant with additional criteria of commercial potential. The peer-review model was thus extended from basic research to follow-on programs to encourage utilization of the results of basic research. Political opposition to government support of industry was largely avoided by encouraging the university to mediate the interaction. The university was the institution of choice in three key instances: agriculture (mid-19th century), the military (World War II), and industry (1970s).

The performance of linearity was improved by introducing expertise in transfer on both sides of the equation. On the university side were people with industrial expertise to find partners in industry, and on the firm side persons with academic expertise, to search universities for useful knowledge and technology. Programs that offer funds to researchers to explore the practical implications of research were introduced and expanded. It was expected that this more systematic approach would produce better results. This series of programs and laws to encourage innovation has gone a long way toward re-creating the wartime interactive model of innovation. Further steps can be taken.

Policy recommendations

1   *Spread entrepreneurial education throughout the university.* When they exist at present, courses in entrepreneurship are typically offered only in the business and engineering schools, and even then separately from each other, losing the opportunities for technical and business students to interact and create new ventures collaboratively. Just as every student learns to write an essay, setting forth ideas and experiences, and a scientific paper, matching evidence to hypotheses, every student should also learn to write a business plan, setting forth objectives and providing a market test of their viability.

2   *Develop network incubators and incubator firms.* When incubators exist they are often isolated entities sponsored by an individual university, municipality, or business firm. Networked incubators have the possibility to encourage firms to undertake joint projects that neither entity could accomplish by itself. A technology platform from a firm in one incubator can be made into a business in another incubator. International incubator networks can give start-ups some of the reach of a multinational firm, helping them to find marketing representatives abroad.

3   *Incentivize regional actors to collaborate and cooperate.* Especially in larger regions where there may be more than one university, multiple governmental units, and several leading firms or clusters, centrifugal forces may keep potential partners apart. National agencies need to be cognizant that the relatively small incentives that may serve to bring triple helix actors together in a small region may not work in

a large region where different groups may compete for leadership status rather than work out an accommodation. On the other hand, they may be willing to accept an invitation to cooperate made by a sufficiently prestigious actor, such as a leading firm in Silicon Valley or the Federal Reserve Bank in New York City.

4   *Create an array of venture capitals.* Overreliance on a single type of venture capital instrument can result in stasis and gaps in fields where traditional funds are not active. Multiple venture capital agents, based on different premises, can create a division of labor in which early-stage and later needs are met as well as social and business goals. A balanced portfolio of venture capital entities is essential to the full economic and social development of a region.

5   *Develop multiple knowledge bases.* Too narrow a knowledge base can leave a region bereft when a technological paradigm runs dry, temporarily or permanently. The availability of alternative knowledge bases gives the region the potential to shift from one technological area to another and avoid gaps. A broad-based university with several critical masses of intellectual activity with potential for capitalization is the basis of a triple helix region that is able to renew itself periodically. The Boston area's shift from the textiles and metalworking industries in the early 20th century to minicomputers in the mid-20th century and currently to biotechnology, based on the breadth of its academic resources, exemplifies this strategy.

6   *Create an entrepreneurial academic entity.* If an entrepreneurial university, interested in the capitalization of knowledge and in playing a leadership role in the economic and social development of its region, does not exist, then it has to be invented. A new university may be founded for this purpose as MIT was in the mid-19th century or Linköping in the late 20th. An existing university may also be encouraged to play this role. Alternatively a group of universities may establish an entrepreneurial unit, like the Stockholm School of Entrepreneurship, to take this role on behalf of a local academic community.

Toward a meta-innovation system

A meta-innovation system comprises multiple sources of initiative, top-down, bottom-up and lateral, to create innovative organizations, firm and non-firm, from elements of the triple helix, in response to the economic and social needs of particular societies. In recent years, the focus of innovation has shifted from the internal organization of the large firm, and its R & D activities, to clusters and high-tech start-ups. Large-firm issues persist as part of broader networks, comprising firms of various scale and scope and other entities. Interaction among university, industry, and government as equal actors is the generative source of innovation in the triple helix.

The shift from a single source of initiative, such as the national government or the firm, to a multiple-source arises from triple helix interactions reinforcing each other and bringing forth new initiatives. In a meta-innovation system, initiatives arise from the bottom up from universities and municipal governments; laterally from industry groups, regional associations, and state governments; and from the top down from national government.

A precondition for a meta-innovation system of multiple sources of initiatives is that the institutional spheres of the triple helix are differentiated and include actors at various levels. Governmental organs and agencies operate at state and municipal levels. Industrial associations have state and municipal branches, with decision-making authority, in addition to their national boards. Federal universities, located in all states of Brazil, have become involved in regional issues while state universities take up national issues.

A second stage of the development of a meta-innovation system is the creation of hybrid entities that are more productive than the individual elements from which they derive. Initiatives from one source are extended by another level or taken in a new direction by an actor in a different institutional sphere. The development of an incubator movement in Brazil, from the triple helix of university, industry, and government, and the transformation of the incubator from its original high-tech focus to a broader role in institution-formation, at various technological levels and beyond the economic sphere, exemplify "meta-innovation."

In a third stage of development multiple actors, from different spheres, formulate and carry out joint projects together such as the development of a software cluster at the municipal level in Brazil. Whereas 30 years ago the science park was instituted in an isolated situation, now it is much more likely to be begun as a cooperative project that is inserted in a dense innovation infrastructure, including incubator networks, entrepreneurship programs, and branches of multinational firms. A failure 30 years ago, apparently due to lack of funds, technology parks are currently successful, despite persisting lack of funds, since they now fit into an organizational continuum.

The European Union has initiated parallel processes and programs.[8] Indeed, the EU and the US borrow innovation formats from each other. Thus the ESPRIT program to encourage software development was a response to the US "Star Wars" initiative. The US Advanced Technology Program attempted to replicate the EU framework programs of encouraging national champions. All of these initiatives have in common the stimulation of networks among the institutional spheres, whether starting from the double helix of government–industry, commonplace in Europe, or the double helix of government–university, more typical in the

US. Over time, as with the Advanced Technology Program, a US anomaly which was built upon an industry–government collaboration, the missing third institutional sphere is brought into the picture.

The future of the triple helix and the triple helix of the future

The triple helix thesis is that the university goes into the future as the predominant organizational format of a knowledge-based society. An industrial organization, whether capitalist or socialist, was presumed to be the dominant form of social organization in producing the goods and services of society. As the knowledge component of the firm is increased, it begins to act more like a university in collaborating, developing, and distributing knowledge.

Marx's assumption that social change was merely a matter of changing control over an existing mode of industrial production, that there would not be new developments in the forces and relations of production, is superseded. The academic laboratory or research group model of intellectual production, of cooperation and collaboration among groups from different institutional spheres, cross-fertilizing each other, is a more productive model than the isolated firm, or even one in an industrial district but without an academic component.

Another basis for change in innovation models is that Max Weber's "iron cage"—the assumption that technology would increase in size and scale, making bureaucratization the sole organizational model in society—has also been disconfirmed. Schumpeter's hypothesis of creative destruction is now accompanied by a process of creative reconstruction of technological and organizational elements into new configurations.[9] Innovation is a broader process than any single institutional sphere or national style. Interaction among the institutional spheres of university, industry, and government, playing both their own traditional roles and each other's, in various combinations, is the basis of societal creativity. The resulting triple helix is a new global system of innovation.

Notes

Introduction

1. Dalley, Stephanie and Peter Oleson. 2003. "Senacherib, Archimedes, and the Water Screw: The Context of Invention in the Ancient World" *Technology and Culture* vol. 44 no. 1, pp. 1–26.
2. Waldrop, M. Mitchell. 2001. *The Dream Machine: J. C. R. Licklider and the Revolution that Made Computing Personal.* New York: Viking. p. 405. In the face of skepticism from the military sponsors of artificial intelligence research in the mid-1970s, the head of the computing office in the Advanced Research Program in the US Defense Department concluded that it would be to the mutual advantage of all for the academic researchers to take an interest in their sponsor's practical problems: "the shift will give the university research groups an engineering arm, a marketplace, customers, users. [That] integration will strengthen the basic work because there will be more feedback from real tests of the big new ideas . . ."
3. Sorlin, Sverker. 2002. "Cultivating the Place of Knowledge" SISTER working paper no. 9, www.sister.nu (last accessed October 16, 2007).
4. See Kornberg, Arthur. 1996. *The Golden Helix: Inside Biotech Ventures.* Sausalito, CA: University Science Books. Dr. Kornberg, a Nobel Prize-winner and self-described pure academic, discusses how he became enthralled by the firm-formation process.

1 Pathways to the triple helix

1. Etzkowitz, Henry. 1983. "Entrepreneurial Scientists and Entrepreneurial Universities in American Academic Science" *Minerva* vol. 21 pp. 198–233.
2. Merton, Robert K. 1979 [1942]. *Sociology of Science.* Chicago: University of Chicago Press.
3. Kornhauser, William. 1962. *Scientists in Industry: Conflict and Accommodation.* Berkeley: University of California Press.
4. Etzkowitz, H. and L. Leydesdorff 2000. "The Dynamics of Innovation: From National Systems and 'Mode 2' to a Triple Helix of University–Industry–Government Relations" *Research Policy* February, vol. 29 pp. 109–123. See also www.triplehelix5.com.
5. Etzkowitz, Henry. 2002. *MIT and the Rise of Entrepreneurial Science.* London: Routledge.
6. Simmel, Georg. 1964. *Conflict and the Web of Group Affiliations.* New York: Free Press.
7. Polanyi, Karl. 1944. *The Great Transformation.* Boston: Beacon Books.

8. Mustar, Philip and Philip Laredo. 2002. "Innovation and Research Policy in France (1980–2000) or the Disappearance of the Colbertist State" *Research Policy* vol. 31 no. 1 pp. 55–72.

9. Melman, Seymour. 1970. *Pentagon Capitalism.* New York: McGraw Hill.

10. Mowery, David, Richard Nelson, Bhaven Sampat, and Aristide Ziedonis. 2004. *Ivory Tower and Industrial Innovation.* Palo Alto: Stanford University Press.

11. Readings, Bill. 1997. *The University in Ruins.* Cambridge, MA: Harvard University Press See also Bok, Derek. 2003. *Universities in the Marketplace: The Commercialization of Higher Education.* Princeton: Princeton University Press; and Krimsky, Sheldon. 2004. *Science in the Private Interest: Has the Lure of Profits Corrupted Biomedical Research?* Lanham, MD: Rowman and Littlefield.

12. Zhou, Chunyan. 2001. "On Science and Technology Field" *Science of Science and Management of S & T* vol. 22 no. 4 pp. 13–15.

13. This section draws upon Etzkowitz, Henry and Chunyan Zhou "Regional Innovation Initiator: The Entrepreneurial University in Various Triple Helix Models" theme paper for Triple Helix VI conference, Singapore May 16–18, 2007; www.triplehelix6.com.

14. Zhou, Chunyan. 2002. *Transforming from Science to Technology: The Scientific Basis of the Technological Era.* Shenyang: Northeastern University Press.

15. Etzkowitz, Henry and Loet Leydesdorff. 2000. "The Dynamics of Innovation: From National Systems and 'Mode 2' to a Triple Helix of University–Industry–Government Relations" *Research Policy* vol. 29 pp. 109–123.

16. Pareto, Vilfredo. 1991 [1901]. *The Rise and Fall of Elites.* New Brunswick, NJ: Transaction Publishers.

17. Mills, C. Wright. 1958. *The Power Elite.* New York: Oxford University Press.

18. Djerassi, Carl. 1992. *The Pill, Pygmys, Chimps, and Degas' Horse.* New York: Basic Books.

19. Törnqvist, Gunnar. 2002. *Science at the Cutting Edge: The Future of the Oresund Region.* Copenhagen: Copenhagen Business School Press.

20. Johnston, Robert and Christopher Edwards. 1987. *Entrepreneurial Science.* Westport, CT: Quorum Books.

21. VanDemark, Brian. 2003. *Pandora's Keepers: Nine Men and the Atomic Bomb.* Boston: Little, Brown.

22. Braun, Ernest and Stuart MacDonald. 1978. *Revolution in Miniature: The History and Impact of Semiconductor Electronics.* Cambridge: Cambridge University Press.

23. Waldrop, M. Michael. 2001. *The Dream Machine: JCR Licklider and the Revolution That Made Computing Personal.* New York: Penguin, p. 405.

24. BBN was considered the "third shop," an equal of Harvard and MIT, in the Cambridge US artificial intelligence community Author interview with Professor Marvin Minsky, Electrical Engineering and Computer Science, MIT, 1986.

25. Hafner, Katie and Matthew Lyon. 1996. *Where Wizards Stay up Late: The Origins of the Internet.* New York: Simon and Schuster.

26. Hoddeson, Lilian and Vicki Daitch. 2002. *True Genius: The Life and Science of John Bardeen.* Washington, DC: Joseph Henry Press. pp. 406–407.

27. Wolff, Kurt H. 1950. *The Sociology of Georg Simmel.* New York: Free Press.

28. Marx, Karl. 1973 [1857]. *The Grundrisse: Foundations of the Critique of Political Economy.* English version, London: Pelican Marx Library.

29. Rossiter, Margaret. 1975. *The Emergence of Agricultural Science*. New Haven: Yale University Press.
30. Weber, Max. 1947. *Theory of Social and Economic Organization*. New York: Oxford University Press.
31. Weber, Max. 1958. *The Protestant Ethic and the Spirit of Capitalism*. New York: Scribners.

2 The entrepreneurial university

1. Karolinska University, Stockholm: www.karolinska.se. Last accessed on October 16, 2007.
2. Machlup, Fritz. 1962. *The Production and Distribution of Knowledge in the United States*. Princeton, NJ: Princeton University Press.
3. Freeman, Christopher and Luc Soete. 1997. *The Economics of Industrial Innovation*. London: Pinter Press. p. 3.
4. See Rothblatt, Sheldon and Bjorn Wittrock (eds.) 1993. *The European and American University since 1800*. Cambridge: Cambridge University Press.
5. Rashdall, Hastings. 1936 [1896]. *Universities of Europe in the Middle Ages*. Oxford: Oxford University Press; Jencks, Christopher and David Riesman. 1968. *The Academic Revolution*. New York: Doubleday; Graham, Hugh Davis, and Nancy Diamond. 1997. *The Rise of American Research Universities: Elites and Challengers in the Postwar Era*. Baltimore, MD: Johns Hopkins University Press.
6. Etzkowitz, Henry. 1983. "Entrepreneurial Scientists and Entrepreneurial Universities in American Academic Science" *Minerva* 21 pp. 198–233.
7. Mills, C. Wright. 1958. *The Power Elite*. New York: Oxford University Press.
8. Herrera, S. 2001. "Academic Research is the Engine of Europe's Biotech Industry" *Red Herring* December. pp. 72–74.
9. See www.AUTM.com. Last accessed October 16, 2007.
10. Viale, Riccardo and Henry Etzkowitz. 2005. "Third Academic Revolution: Polyvalent Knowledge; The 'DNA' of the Triple Helix" in *Triple Helix 5*. Turin, Italy.www.triplehelix5.com. Last accessed October 16, 2007.
11. Mowery, David, Richard Nelson, Bhaven Sampat, and Aristide Ziedonis 2004. *Ivory Tower and Industrial Innovation: University–Industry Technology Transfer Before and After the Bayh-Dole Act*. Stanford: Stanford University Press.
12. Shimshoni, Daniel. 1970. "The mobile scientist in the American instrument industry" *Minerva* 8 pp. 59–89.
13. Gustin, Bernard. 1975. "The Emergence of the German Chemical Profession 1790–1867" PhD thesis, University of Chicago.
14. Etzkowitz, Henry. 2002. *MIT and the Rise of Entrepreneurial Science*. London: Routledge.
15. For a report on survey research on this phenomenon in one academic discipline, molecular biology, see David Blumenthal et al. 1986. "Industrial Support of University Research in Biotechnology" *Science* 231 pp. 242–246.
16. Clark, Burton. 1999. *Creating Entrepreneurial Universities: Organizational Pathways of Transformation*. New York: Pergamon.
17. Campbell, Katherine. 2002. "Global Investing: Moving beyond the Silicon Valley: Europe's High-Tech Centres Differ from Their US Cousins." FT.com. Last accessed October 16, 2007. See also *ACM TechNews* vol. 4 no. 301 January 18, 2002 "Moving beyond the Silicon Valley Model": "European high-tech clusters are following a very different model from Silicon Valley, and they seem to be the better for it. Silicon Valley has been characterized by

an overabundance of capital, a dynamic environment, and a large domestic market." http://www.acm.org/technews/articles/2002-4/0118f.html#item3.
18. Mills, C. Wright. 1958. *The Power Elite*. New York: Oxford University Press.
19. Graham, Loren. 1998. *What Have We Learned about Science and Technology from the Russian Experience?* Palo Alto: Stanford University Press. p. 129.

3 The evolution of the firm

1. O'Boyle, Thomas. 1998. *At Any Cost: Jack Welch, General Electric and the Pursuit of Profit*. New York: Random House.
2. Mckelvey, Maureen. 1994. "Evolutionary Innovation: Early Industrial Uses of Genetic Engineering" (PhD dissertation) Linköping: Linköping University.
3. Lowegren, Marie. 2003. "New Technology-Based Forms in Science Parks," (PhD dissertation). Lund Institute of Economic Research: Lund University.
4. Gray, Colin. 1998. *Enterprise and Culture*. London: Routledge.
5. Tournatzky, Louis, Paul Waugoman and Denis Gray. 2002. *Innovation U.: New University Roles in a Knowledge Economy*. Research Triangle Park, NC: Southern Growth Policies Board.
6. Etzkowitz, Henry, Magnus Gulbrandsen and Janet Levitt. 2000. *Public Venture Capital: Government Funding Sources for Technology Entrepreneurs*. New York: Harcourt.
7. Magnuson, Lars. 2000. *An Economic History of Sweden*. London: Routledge.
8. Stix, Gary. 2003. "Reverse-Engineering Clinical Biology" *Scientific American* February pp. 28–30.
9. Spulber, Daniel. 1999. *Market Microstructure: Intermediaries and the Theory of the Firm*. Cambridge: Cambridge University Press.
10. Chandler, Alfred. 1962. *Strategy and Structure: Chapters in the History of American Industrial Enterprise*. Cambridge, MA: MIT Press.
11. Storper, Michael. 1997. *The Regional World: Territorial Development in a Global Economy*. New York: Guilford Press.
12. Klofsten, Magnus. 1994. "Technology-Based Firms: Critical Aspects of their Early Development" *Journal of Enterprising Culture* vol. 2 no. 1 pp. 535–557.
13. Saxenian, Annalee. 1994. *Regional Advantage*. Cambridge, MA: Harvard University Press.
14. Nonaka, Ikujiro and Hirotaka Takeuchi. 1995. *The Knowledge-Creating Company*. New York: Oxford University Press.
15. Schumpeter, Joseph. 1942. *Capitalism, Socialism, and Democracy*. New York: Harper.
16. Etzkowitz, Henry and Magnus Klofsten, 2005. "The Innovating Region: Towards a Theory of Knowledge Based Regional Development" *Research Management* vol. 35 no. 3 pp. 243–255.

4 The optimum role of government

1. Benner, Mats. 2003. "The Scandinavian Challenge: The Future of Advanced Welfare States in the Knowledge Economy" *Acta Sociologica* vol. 46 no. 2 pp. 132–149.
2. See Greyson, Leslie. 2002. "Give Us Back Our Regions" *Innovation Policy Review* vol. 4 no. 2 April p. 1.
3. Walshok, Mary. 1995. *Knowledge without Boundaries*. San Francisco: Jossey Bass.
4. Etzkowitz, Henry. 1997. "From Zero-Sum to Value-Added Strategies: The

Emergence of Knowledge-Based Industrial Policy in the States of the United States" *Policy Studies Journal* vol. 25 no. 3 pp. 412–424.
5. Sapolsky, Harvey. 1990. *Science and the Navy: The History of the Office of Naval Research*. Princeton, NJ: Princeton University Press.
6. Etzkowitz, Henry. 2002. *MIT and the Rise of Entrepreneurial Science*. London: Routledge.
7. Etzkowitz, Henry, Magnus Gulbrandsen and Janet Levitt. 2001. *Public Venture Capital*. New York: Aspen/Kluwer.
8. Crouch, Colin. 1993. *Industrial Relations and European State Traditions*. Oxford: Oxford University Press.
9. See "An Asian Tiger's Bold Experiment" *Science* 316 pp. 38–41. Published April 6, 2007. www.sciencemag.org. Last accessed October 16, 2007.

5 Regional innovation

1. Koepp, Rob. 2002. *Clusters of Creativity: Enduring Lessons on Innovation and Entrepreneurship from Silicon Valley and Europe's Silicon Fen*. New York: John Wiley.
2. Sassen, Saskia. 2001. *The Global City: New York, London, and Tokyo*. Princeton: Princeton University Press.
3. Albrechts, L. et al. 1989. *Regional Policy at the Crossroads: European Perspectives*. London: Jessica Kingsley.
4. Heydebrand, Wolf. 1999. "Multimedia Networks, Globalization and Strategies of Innovation: The Case of Silicon Alley" in Hans-Joachim Brazcyck et al. (eds.) *Multimedia and Regional Economic Restructuring*. London: Routledge.
5. See Stokes, Donald. 1997. *Pasteur's Quadrant*. Washington, DC: The Brookings Institution.
6. Casas, Rosalba, Rebeca de Gortari, and Josefa Santos Ma. 1999. "The Building of Knowledge Spaces in Mexico: A Regional Approach to Networking" *Research Policy* vol. 29 no. 2 pp. 225–241.
7. Zachary, G. Pascal. 2002. "Ghana's digital dilemma. Technology Review." http://www.technologyreview.com/articles/02/07/zachary0702.asp?p=1. Last accessed October 16, 2007.
8. Etzkowitz, Henry. 2002. *MIT and the Rise of Entrepreneurial Science*. London: Routledge, p. 108.
9. Saxenian, A. 1994. *Regional Advantage*. Cambridge, MA: Harvard University Press.
10. Hamel, Gary. 1999. "Bringing Silicon Valley Inside" *Harvard Business Review*, September–October, pp. 71–84.
11. Cooke, P. 2002. "Regional Innovation Systems: General Findings and Some New Evidence from Biotechnology Clusters" *Journal of Technology Transfer* 27 pp. 133–145.
12. Hofmaier, Bernard. 2001. "Learning Regions—Concepts, Visions and Examples" Halmstadt University College http://www.hh.se/hss/Papers/papers/hofmaier.pdf. Last accessed October 16, 2007.

6 Triple helix technopolis

1. Culliton, Barbara. 1982. "The Academic Industrial Complex" *Science* vol. 216 pp. 960–962.
2. Rosenberg, Nathan. 1994. *Exploring the Black Box: Technology, Economics and History*. Cambridge: Cambridge University Press. See also Asner, Glen "The Linear Model, the US Department of Defense and the Golden Age of Industrial Research" in Karl Grandin, Nina Wormbs, and Sven Widmalm

(eds.). 2004. *The Science–Industry Nexus: History, Policy, Implications.* Sagamore Beach, MA: Science History Publications.

3. TechnoL Listserve, January 14, 2005. http://www.techno-l.org/. Last accessed October 16, 2007.
4. Interview with Dr. da Silva, director, Porto Digital Recife, Brazil, June 2002.
5. See Etzkowtitz, Henry and Carol Kemelgor. 1998. "The Role of Centres in the Collectivisation of Academic Science" *Minerva* vol. 36 no. 3 pp. 231–268.
6. Lowen, Rebecca. 1997. *Creating the Cold War University: The Transformation of Stanford.* Stanford: Stanford University Press.
7. Interview with Pierre Lafitte, founder of Sophia Antipolis, Nice, France, 1995.
8. Interview with Dr. da Silva, director, Porto Digital Recife, Brazil, June 2002.

7 The incubation of innovation

1. Israel, Paul. 1998. *Edison: A Life of Invention.* New York: John Wiley.
2. Hansen, Morton, Henry Chesbrugh, and Nita Donald Sull. 2000. "Networked Incubators: Hothouse of the New Economy" *Harvard Business Review*, September–October pp. 74–84.
3. Rice, Mark and Jana Matthews. 1995. *Growing New Ventures, Creating New Jobs: Principles and Practices of Successful Business Incubation.* Kansas City, MO: Kauffman Center for Entrepreneurial Leadership. See also Kalis, Nanette. 2001. *Technology Commercialization through New Company Formation: Why US Universities Are Incubating Companies.* Athens, OH: NBIA Publications.
4. Colombo, Massimo and March Delmastro. 2002. "How Effective Are Technology Incubators? Evidence from Italy" *Research Policy* vol. 31 pp. 1103–1122, p. 1120. See also Sternberg, R. 1990. "The Impact of Innovation Centers on Small Technology-Based Firms: The Example of the Federal Republic of Germany" *Small Business Economics* 2, 105–118.
5. Knopp, Linda. 2003. "NBIA Honors Excellence in Business Incubation" May 19. www.nbia.org. Last accessed October 16, 2007.
6. International Association of Science Parks. 2002. www.iasp.ws. Last accessed October 16, 2007. For additional information on international incubation, see World Conference on Business Incubation (www.wcbi.com). For examples of national associations, see ANPROTEC (Brazil) www.anprotec.org.br/. Last accessed October 16, 2007. National Business Incubation Association (NBIA) (US) www.nbia.org. Last accessed October 16, 2007.
7. Lalkaka, Rustram. 2000. *Rapid Growth of Business Incubation in China: Lessons for Developing and Restructuring Countries.* World Association of Technological and Research Organizations (WAITRO), Taastrup, Denmark: Danish Technological Institute.
8. Leslie, Stuart W. and Robert H. Kargon. 1996. "Selling Silicon Valley: Frederick Terman's Model for Regional Advantage" *Business History Review* Winter pp. 435–472.
9. See www.apoio.inf.br/tecsoft/default.htm. Last accessed October 16, 2007.
10. See www.nbia.org. Last accessed October 16, 2007.
11. Etzkowitz, Henry, Jose Mello, and Mariza Almeida. 2005. "Towards 'Meta-Innovation' in Brazil: The Evolution of the Incubator and the Emergence of a Triple Helix," *Research Policy* vol. 34 no. 4 pp. 411–424.

8 Reinventing venture capital

1. Indeed, two recent reports from the National Bureau of Economic Research and the National Research Council document that the Advanced Technology Program has been highly successful in producing technological innovation. See "ATP Garners Praise in Two New Studies" *Technology Access Report* March 2003 vol. 16 no. 2 pp. 2–3. There are smart people in government, some of whom have had a long-term and highly perceptive view of technological futures and business opportunities. For example, the support of Joseph Licklider, DARPA program officer for the creation of computer networks that later became the Internet and former Vice President Gore's advocacy of information highways, exemplify the efficacy of government's role as public venture capitalist. See Hafner, Katie and Matthew Lyon. 1996. *When Wizards Stay up Late: The Origins of the Internet.* New York: Simon and Schuster.
2. Gompers, Paul and Josh Lerner. 2002. *The Venture Capital Cycle.* Cambridge, MA: MIT Press.
3. Interview with Jorge Avila, director of Innovar, Rio de Janeiro, 2000. See also www.finep.gov.br Last accessed October 16, 2007.
4. Discussion between representatives of Yozma and FinnLombarda at the Finance and Knowledge Workshop, Milan, Italy, November 2001.
5. Sergio Campo dall'Orto, professor and incubator director, Milan Polytechnic, interviews with the author, 1996, 2000, and 2002.
6. Etzkowitz, Henry, Magnus Gulbrandsen, and Janet Levitt. 2001. *Public Venture Capital.* 2nd edition. New York: Aspen/Kluwer.
7. See Salmen Kaita, Jukka-Pekka and Ahti Salo. 2002. "Rationales for Government Intervention in the Commercialization of New Technologies" *Technology Analysis and Strategic Management* vol. 14. no. 2 June pp. 183–200.
8. Andretsch, David B., Albert Link, and John Scott, 2002. "Public/Private Technology Partnerships: Evaluating SBIR Supported Research" *Research Policy* vol. 31 no. 1 pp. 145–158.
9. Etzkowitz, Henry, Magnus Gulbrandsen, and Janet Levitt. 2001. *Public Venture Capital.* 2nd edition. New York: Aspen/Kluwer.
10. Anonymous. 2002."Signs of the Times: Start-Ups Starved for Cash while VC Coffers Stay Locked" *Technology Access Report* vol. 15 no. 6 July p. 16.
11. Feldman, Maryann et al. 2002. "Equity and the Technology Transfer Strategies of American Universities" *Management Science* vol. 48 no. 1 pp. 105–121. See also "VCs Take to Tech Transfer" *Technology Access Report* February 2003 vol. 16 no. 1 pp. 1–2 for a discussion of renewed private venture capital interest in US university spin-off firms.
12. Gompers, Paul and Josh Lerner. 2002. *The Venture Capital Cycle.* Cambridge, MA: MIT Press.
13. Barrow, Colin. 2001. *Incubators: A Realist's Guide to the World's New Business Accelerators.* New York: John Wiley.
14. Lars Ojefors, Director of Industrifonden, interview with the author, Stockholm, 2002.
15. See www.cdvca.org. Last accessed October 16, 2007.
16. Van Osnabrugge, Mark and Robert Robertson. 2000. *Angel Investing.* San Francisco: Jossey Bass.
17. Van Looy, Bart, Liana Marina Ranga, Julie Callaert, Koenraad Debackere, and Edwin Zimmermann. "Combining entrepreneurial and scientific performance in academia: Towards a compounded and reciprocal Matthew-effect?" *Research Policy* 2004, vol. 33 no. 3, pp. 425–441.
18. See Wilson, John. 1986. *The New Venturers: Inside the High-Stakes World of Venture Capital.* Boston: Addison Wesley for a discussion of the "nurtur-

ing role" played by venture capitalists in helping attract talent and devising strategy.

9 The endless transition

1. Bush, Vannevar. 1945. *Science: The Endless Frontier*. Washington, DC: US Government Printing Office.
2. Collins, Randall and Joseph Ben David. 1966. "Social Factors in the Origins of a New Science: The Case of Psychology" *American Sociological Review* vol. 31 no. 4 pp. 451–65.
3. Gibbons, Michael et al. 1994. *The New Production of Knowledge*. Beverly Hills: Sage. See also Nowotny, Helga, Peter Scott, and Michael Gibbons. 2001. *Rethinking Science: Knowledge and the Public in an Age of Uncertainty*. London: Polity Press.
4. Storr, Richard J. 1968. *Harper's University*. Chicago: University of Chicago Press.
5. Storr, Richard. 1953. *The Beginnings of Graduate Education in America*. Chicago: University of Chicago Press.
6. See Hollinger, David. 1995. "Science as a Weapon in the United States during and after World War II" *Isis* 86 pp. 440–454; Wang, Jessica. 1999. "Merton's Shadow: Perspectives on Science and Democracy" *Historical Studies in the Physical Sciences* 30 pp. 280–306.
7. Bush, Vannevar. 1945. *Science: The Endless Frontier*. Washington, DC: US Government Printing Office.
8. Claryssse, B. and U. Muldur. 2002. "Regional Cohesion in Europe? An Analysis of How EU Public RTD Support Influences the Techno-economic Landscape" *Research Policy* vol. 30 no. 2 pp. 275–296.
9. See Mingers, John. 2002. "Can Social Systems Be Autopoietic?" *Sociological Review* vol. 50 no. 2 pp. 278–299 for a discussion of radical change and development in a social system without loss of identity. "This is rather common in the social world where we see many groupings—families, companies, religions, cultures, and societies—that exhibit long-term stability and persistence despite enormous changes in their environment, and their own internal membership and structure" (p. 281).

Index

Note: page numbers in *italic* refer to figures and tables.

Abetti, Pier 107
academic entrepreneurship 30, 39–40;
  universalization of 30–31
Academy of Engineering, Stockholm
  62
Advanced Research Program 149 n. 2
Advanced Technology Program (ATP)
  70, 71–72, 128, 146–147, 154 n. 1
Africa 2, 31, 79
Aho, Esko 2
American Research and Development
  (ARD) 108, 122, 123–125, 130,
  136
angel investors/angel syndicates 31,
  52, 62, 63, 88, 133–134
ANPROTEC 11, 114, 154 n. 6
Apple Computer 131
Appropriation Act, NIH 128
ARD *see* American Research and
  Development
Arthur D. Little 95
assisted linear innovation model 4, 38,
  73, 137, 139
Association of University Related
  Research Parks 100
ATP *see* Advanced Technology
  Program
Audubon Park, Manhattan 102

Bacon, Francis 139
Bardeen, John 24
Bayh-Dole Act (1980) 39–40, 92–93,
  95
Baylor University Medical School 130
BBN *see* Bolt, Beranek, and Newman

biotechnology industry 31, 52, 83,
  124; Cambridge, Massachusetts
  87–88
Blekinge Institute of Technology,
  Sweden 38–39
Bolt, Beranek, and Newman (BBN)
  24, 150 n. 24
Bose, A. 22
Boston University 130
Bothnian Arc, Finland/Sweden 76
Brazil 2, 12, 81, 102; entrepreneurial
  education 31; FINEP 120, 126–127;
  incubator movement 11, 29, 49,
  62–63, 109, 110, 113–114, 116,
  146; SOFTEC 115; and statist
  model 14
Brazilian National Development
  Agency (FINEP) 120, 126–127
Brookhaven National Laboratory 83
Bush, Vannevar 23, 35, 67, 86, 139,
  142–143

Cadena, Gustavo 120
California Proposition 71: 17
capitalization of knowledge *see*
  knowledge capitalization
Casa, Rosalba 7
Cascadia, British Columbia 76
CDFI *see* Community Development
  Financial Institutions Fund
Center for Business and Policy Studies,
  Stockholm 5
Center for Innovation and
  Entrepreneurship, Linköping 84
center-formation 96–98

CESAR, University of Recife, Brazil 95–96
Chalmers University Science Park, Gothenburg 101
China 110
civil society 11, 62–63, 74
classical social theory 24–26
Cold War 139
collective entrepreneurship 2
Columbia University Medical School 102
Community Development Financial Institutions Fund (CDFI) 133
community development venture capital 133
Compaq corporation 44
Compton, Karl 20, 86
computer science 31, 32
conferences: and information-sharing 40
conflicts of interest 17–18; and institutional cross-fertilization 21–22
confluence of interest 17–18
CONNECT networking format 62
Connecticut Innovation Agency 128
consensus space 78–79, *81*
contractual firms 50
Control Data 108
COPPE (Graduate School of Engineering, Federal University of Rio de Janeiro) 113
corporate incubation 108–109
corporate venture capital 131–132
corporatism 72
cross-fertilization 21–22, 46
crossover 17, 49, 55, 90, 104
culture: and transfer of venture capital models 127

DARPA *see* Defense Advanced Research Projects Agency
Data General 87
DEC *see* Digital Equipment Corporation
Defense Advanced Research Projects Agency (DARPA) 23–24, 71, 143
Denmark: investment in incubator firms 120; Oresund 23, 76, 80
Digital Equipment Corporation (DEC) 87, 99, 125
direct innovation policy 60–61
discipline hybridization 141–142
discontinuous innovation 89

Djerassi, Carl 22
Doriot, Georges 136
Downtown Partnership, New York 81
"dual life" individuals 55–56

Edison, Thomas Alva: "invention factory" 107
Electrum Foundation, Kista 103
Entelos 49
entrepreneurial academic model 41
entrepreneurial education 31, 120, 144
entrepreneurial incubators 108
entrepreneurial training 2–3
entrepreneurial universities 27–42, 102, 145; Africa 31; Brazil 31; and capitalization of knowledge 1, 9, 27, 28, 41, 145; as driver of triple helix 29; fully-fledged 38–39; and incubation 111–112; origins of 33–34; transitional 38
entrepreneurs: as RIO 30–31; technology 45–46
entrepreneurship 2–3; academic 39–40; collective 2; individual 2; student 84
Ericsson, Stockholm 99, 103
ESPRIT program 146
European Union (EU) 89, 146; and regional renewal 76
extra-networking 112, 114
Exxon 131

Federal University of Fluminense (UFF) 79, 113–114
Federal University of Rio de Janeiro 113
FINEP *see* Brazilian National Development Agency
Finland 60, 76
firm-formation 48; collaboration and 46; incubators and 110–111; projects 37, 44; role of universities in 49
firms: evolution of 49–52
Ford, Henry 51
forward innovation model 99–100, 143
foundation venture capital 132–133
Framework Programs (EU) 71
France: Sophia Antipolis 99–100; and statist model 14–15
free-rider problems 39–40

Gates, Bill 44, 47
General Electric Corporation 107, 108
General Motors (GM) 51
George Mason University 88
Germany 33–34
Glaxo-Welcome 99
government: fundamental role of 9; and laissez-faire model 12, 15, 16; optimum role of 59–74; as RIO 85; role in laissez-faire society 69–70; statist model of 12, 14–15, 16
government–industry relations 67–68
government technology development awards 53, 54
government–university relations 66–67
Guedes, Mauricio 113

Harvard 33, 37
Health Information Initiative 71
Helsinki 60
Hewlett Packard, Palo Alto 87
Hodges, Luther 85
Honduras 118
Humboldtian academic model 10
hybridization 41

IBM, Research Triangle Park, North Carolina 85
Idealab 109
In-Q-tel 127
incentive system 144–145
incremental innovation 89
incubation: concept of 109; corporate 108–109; entrepreneurial universities and 111–112; of innovation 106; networked 112; origin and development of 106–109; principles of 118–119
incubator movement 9, 11, 37; Brazil 11, 29, 49, 62–63, 109, 110, 113–114, 116, 146; Mexico 63
incubators: contemporary model 111; development of 119–121; entrepreneurial 108; and firm-formation 110; incubation of 117–118; and organizational technology transfer 114–115; private (networked) 109, 112–113, 144; and university's educational mission 105
independence 41

indirect industrial policy 63–65
individual entrepreneurship 2
Industrifonden 132–133
industry: fundamental role of 9
industry–government relations 67–68
information networks 22–23
information-sharing 97–98, 104; through publications 40, 94–95, 97
INNOVA 120
innovation 4, 8, 9, 42; cross-fertilization and 46; discontinuous 89; incremental 89; incubation of 106; initiatives 91; meta-innovation system 145–147; netlike 24; nonlinear 23–24; regional 75–89; triple helix model 7–8
innovation models: assisted linear 4, 38, 73, 137, 139; forward 99–100, 143; linear 4, 38, 60, 73, 80, 137, 138–139; reverse linear 80, 100–101, 138
innovation organizers (IO) 8, 103
innovation paradox 42, 65
innovation policies: indirect industrial 63–65; Sweden 61–62; US 65–66
innovation space 80–81; creation of *81*
innovation state: basic precepts 73
innovation systems integrator: technology transfer offices as 93–95
institutional cross-fertilization: and conflicts of interest 21–22
intellectual property 17, 27, 37; rights 10, 38, 39–40; universities and 73, 92–93
inter-networking 112, 113–114
interdependence 41
interdisciplinarity 97, 142
Internet 117, 129; 1990s' bubble 125
intra-networking 112–113
"invention factory" (Edison) 107
IO *see* innovation organisers
Ionics 123–124
Israel 126, 127; MAGNET incubator program 120
Italy 58, 127, 110

Japan 15–16, 50
Joint Venture Silicon Valley, California 12, 72, 78–79

Karlskronna University, Sweden 88
Kista Information Technology University, Stockholm 103

Kista Science Park, Stockholm 99, 103

KK *see* Knowledge Competency Foundation

Klofsten, Magnus 3

knowledge 31–32, 145

knowledge-based firms 44, 50, 52: and "dual life" individuals 55; human capital factors 56–57; material factors 57; organizational factors 57

knowledge-based regions 76, 80

knowledge capitalization 20, 133, 140–141; universities and 1, 9, 27, 28, 41, 145

Knowledge Circle, Amsterdam 12

knowledge commercialization: American model 44–45; government role in 46–47; at MIT 45

Knowledge Competency Foundation (KK), Sweden 127, 132

knowledge production 140–141

knowledge space 77–78; creation of 81

Kodak 131

Lafitte, Pierre 99

laissez-faire society 12–13, 15–18, 19–20, 59; government role in 69–70

lateral social mobility 21

Launchpad 39: 109

learning regions 89

Licklider, J. C. R. 24, 154 n. 1

Liebig, Justus 120–121

linear innovation model 4, 38, 60, 73, 80, 137, 138–139

linearity 143–144

Linköping, Sweden 58, 75, 84

Linköping University, Sweden 3

Lisbon Agenda 89

Lund University, Sweden 61

MAGNET incubator program, Israel 120

Manhattan Project 14

Marburger, John 83

market failure 16

market-oriented firms 52–53, 54–55

Markle Foundation 132

Marx, Karl 24, 25, 147

Massachusetts Institute of Technology *see* MIT

Medicon Valley Academy, Sweden 61, 76

Merton, Robert K. 140, 142

Mesopotamia 1

Mexico 59, 103; decentralization of laboratories 77–78; incubator movement 63; intellectual property rights 93

Microsoft Corporation 47, 141

Mills, C. Wright 22

MIT (Massachusetts Institute of Technology) 10, 35, 37, 86, 97; entrepreneurial initiatives 33; knowledge commercialization at 45

Monterrey, Mexico 103

multinational firms 51

nanotechnology 32, 124

National Autonomous University of Mexico (UNAM) 7, 120

National Bureau of Economic Research 154 n. 1

National Business Incubator Association (NBIA) 110, 115, 154 n. 6

National Institute of Health (NIH), US 127, 128

National Research Council 154 n. 1

National Science Foundation (NSF) 4–5, 67, 68, 96, 97, 100, 127

National Technical University, Norway 115

Native American communities: venture capital in 133

NATO Science Policy Workshop, Nice 99

NBIA *see* National Business Incubator Association

Netherlands, The 12

netlike innovation 24

networks 80–81: incubators 112, 116

New England Council 12, 72, 76, 78–79; invention of venture capital firm 80

new technology-based firms (NTBFs) 110

New York Academy of Sciences 20, 79

New York harbor 76

New York Software Industry Association 127–128

New York State Centers Program 83

Newcastle University: Business School 5; professors-of-practice (PoP) scheme 17–18
NIH *see* National Institute of Health
Niteroi Technopole, Brazil 12
Nokia, Finland 60
non-linear innovation 23–24
Norway 115
NSF *see* National Science Foundation

Office of Naval Research (ONR) 143
Office of Scientific Research and Development (OSRD) 66, 142–143
Oresund, Denmark/Sweden 23, 76, 80

PARC Lab 44
Pasteur, Louis 140
patents 86, 94–95
Perkins, William Henry 25
Perry, William 22
Pharmacia Corporation, Uppsala, Sweden 81
Pittsburgh High-tech Council 12
Polytechnico Milan 58, 118, 127
polyvalent knowledge 31–32
Pontifical Catholic University of Rio de Janeiro (PUC) 2, 48: "Project Genesis" 49
PoP scheme *see* professors-of-practice (PoP) scheme
Porto Digital Science Park, Recife 102, 103
Portugal 82
private capital: government guarantees and 73
private incubators 109; intra-networking 112–113
private venture capital 46; scale and scope in 124–125; in US 128–129
professors-of-practice (PoP) scheme 17–18
"Project Genesis": Pontifical Catholic University, Rio de Janeiro 49
public–private partnerships 71–72
public venture capital 7, 46, 125–129; and assisted linear model of innovation 73; government and 63; in "high-state" society 126–127; in "low-state" society 126, 127–129; in Sweden 127; in US 127–128
publications: and information sharing 40, 94–95, 97
PUC *see* Pontifical Catholic University of Rio de Janeiro

R & D: budget increases 69; postwar paradigm 66–67
R & D units: and incubator concept 108; in science parks 99, 101; Volvo 101
Radar Counter-Measures Lab, Harvard 86
RAND Corporation 39
reciprocity 23
reflexivity 41
regional identities 76
regional innovation 75–89; consensus space 77, 78–79; innovation space 77, 80–81; knowledge space 77–78; triple helix spaces 76–77, 81–82
regional innovation initiators (RII) 20
regional innovation organizers (RIO) 19–20, 82; entrepreneurs as 84–85; government as 85; universities as 83–84
regional triple helix: creation of 87–88
Renssellear Polytechnic Institute (RPI) 37, 107
research: commercialization of 31, 32; politicization of location of 41; translational 32
Research Corporation 16–17
research grants 7
research-oriented firms 52–54
Research Triangle Park, North Carolina 85; IBM 85
research universities: Brazil 62; German state governments and 33–34
return on investment (ROI): technology transfer offices and 94
reverse linear innovation model 80, 100–101, 138
Rhone Poulenc 99
RII *see* regional innovation initiators
RIO *see* regional innovation organizers
River Rouge Plant 51
Rogers, William Barton 86
ROI *see* return on investment
Route 128, Boston 80, 85–86, 87
Rowland, Henry 139, 142
Royal Technological University, Stockholm 103
RPI *see* Renssellear Polytechnic Institute

S & T policy *see* science and
   technology policy
Saab Aerospace 84
Saab medical devices 58
Sabato, Jorge 14
San Pedro Sula, Honduras 118
Saxenian, AnnaLee 87
SBIR *see* Small Business Innovation
   Research
Schumpeter, Joseph 52, 147
Science: The Endless Frontier (1945
   report) 142
science and technology (S & T)
   agencies 64
science and technology (S & T) policy
   74; earmarks 72; New York State
   83
science-based economic development
   75: and triple helix spaces 81–82
science parks 90, 146; and
   entrepreneurial universities 38–39;
   forward linear model 99–100;
   and founding of entrepreneurial
   universities 103; ideology v. reality
   101–102; renewal of 98–99; reverse
   linear model 100–101
scientific research, legitimation of
   139–140
SEMATECH 63
Shockley, William Bradford 22
Silicon Alley, New York City 76
Silicon Valley 23, 64, 80, 85–86, 87,
   151 n. 17; firm-formation in 75, 82;
   Joint Venture Silicon Valley 12, 72,
   78–79; Xerox 131
Simmel, Georg 24–25
Singapore 59
Skåne, Sweden 61
Sloan, Alfred P. 51
Small Business Innovation
   Development Act (1982) 68
Small Business Innovation Research
   (SBIR) 68–69, 128, 143–144;
   preliminary program 83
Smart Valley project 78
SMEs (small- and medium-sized firms)
   57
social mobility: lateral 21
Soft Center science park, Karlskronna
   Ronneby, Sweden 38–39
SOFTEC, Brazil 115
Sophia Antipolis, France 99–100
SRI International: Competitiveness
   Center 78

SSBGG (stasis, shortfall, balance,
   gluttony, gap) venture capital cycle
   134–135
standards 49–50
Stanford University 22, 82, 110;
   collaborative innovation strategies
   45; Engineering School 47;
   entrepreneurial initiatives 33;
   science park 87, 98
State of Rio de Janeiro Industry
   Association 79
State University of New York (SUNY),
   Albany 83, 111–112, 114; Stony
   Brook 83–84, 120
State University of Rio de Janeiro at
   Friburgo 79
statist ("high-state") societies 12–15,
   19–20, 59; direct innovation policy
   and 60
Stockholm School of Entrepreneurship
   145
Stony Brook, SUNY 83, 120;
   Biotechnology Center 83–84
Straits Times, Singapore 72–73
Strategic Foundation, Sweden 127
student entrepreneurship 84
SUNY *see* State University of New
   York
Sweden 3, 5, 60–61; Bothnian Arc
   76; holding-company initiative
   73; innovation policy 61–62;
   integration of research policy with
   regional policy 77; intellectual
   property rights 38; Karlskronna
   University 88; Lund University
   61; Medicon Valley Academy 61,
   76; Oresund 23, 76, 80; public
   venture capital in 127; rise in firm-
   formation 48; Saab medical devices
   58; science parks 38–39; Skåne
   61; student entrepreneurship 84;
   technology bridge foundations 61
Symbion, Copenhagen 114–115

Tampere, Finland 60
tax incentives 73
technology-based firms 51
technology bridge foundations 61
technology entrepreneurs 45–46
technology transfer 67: Bayh-Dole Act
   and 39–40, 92–93, 95; international
   115–117; organizational 114–115;
   statist society and 14; universities
   and 19, 31, 36–37

technology transfer offices 90, 91–95; creation of 45; emergence of 91–93; as innovation systems integrator 93–95; and return on investment (ROI) 94

Tennessee Valley watershed 76

Terman, Frederick 83, 86, 114

Texas Instrument 44

3M 131–132

triple helix: circulation 20–22; and civil society 62–63, 74; and classical social theory 24–26; entrepreneurial universities as driver of 29; field theory 18–20; governance in 103–104; interaction model *19*; synthetic interaction model *20*; wartime 66

triple helix firms 44–58, *50*; in "high-state" societies *59*; in "low-state" societies *59*

triple helix model 7–8: bilateral interactions 10; international development of 9; regional development of 8–9; trilateral interactions 10–11

triple helix regions 85–87; creation of 87–88

triple helix spaces: regional 76–77, 81–82; and science-based economic development 81–82

triple helix technopolis 90–104; innovation initiatives, convergence of 91; science parks, renewal of 98–99; technology transfer offices 91–95

triple helix water screw 1

UFF *see* Federal University of Fluminense

UNAM *see* National Autonomous University of Mexico

United States of America: Advanced Technology Program 70, 71–72, 128, 146–147, 154 n. 1; antitrust rules 16; Department of Defense 23–24, 149 n. 2; Department of the Treasury 133; entrepreneurial universities 30–31; innovation policy 65–66; and Japan, competition with 15–16; laissez-faire model 15; policy sciences PhD program 38–39; and statist model 14, 16; venture capital in 128–129

univalent knowledge 32

universities: entrepreneurial 145; as entrepreneurs 37; firm-formation 33; fundamental role of 9; Humboldtian reform 30; incubator facilities 104; and knowledge capitalization 27; land grant 33; and lateral circulation 21; liberal-arts 33; research 30, 33; as RIO 83–84; role of, in firm-formation projects 49; and technology transfer 19; technology transfer in 36–37; technology transfer offices 31, 37, 40; *see also* entrepreneurial universities

university–government relations 23, 66–67: growth of 10; one-fifth rule 10

university–industry relations 95–96: development of 34–37

University of Aveiro, Portugal 82

University of Colorado, Boulder 100–101, 105

University of Columbia 130

University of Giessen, Germany 120–121

University of Nice 99

University of Recife, Brazil: CESAR 95–96

University of Utah 100

University of Zambia: Computer Centre 2

university venture capital 129–130

Uppsala University, Sweden 81

US Army: research funding 67

"valley of death" concept 42, 45–46

venture capital 9, 45, 122–136, 145; angel investors/angel syndicates 133–134; community development 133; corporate 131–132; countercyclical 135; foundation 132–133, 136; objectives 122, 123; private 124–125, 136; public 125–129, 136; typology of 129–134; university 129–130, 136

venture capital cycle (SSBGG) 134–135

venture capital firms: invention of 37, 108

venture capital industry: Brazil 42; UK 42; US 42

Virginia Polytechnic Institute, Blacksburg 88

Volvo 101
Washington, DC 88
Washington State: Cascadia 76
Weber, Max 24, 25, 147
World Innovation Network (WIN)
    115–117

Xerox 44, 109, 131

Yale Science Park 102
Yozma, Israel 126, 127

Zambia 2